GETTYSBURG'S
Forgotten Cavalry Actions

To Jerry Klusewitz,
With very best wishes
to an old friend,

by
Eric J. Wittenberg

[signature]

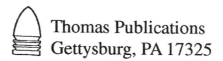

Thomas Publications
Gettysburg, PA 17325

Copyright ©1998 Eric J. Wittenberg

Publisher — Cataloging-in-Publication Data
Wittenberg, Eric J.
  Gettysburg's Forgotten Cavalry Actions / Eric J. Wittenberg
  144 pp.   14 x 21.6 cm.
  Includes index, bibliography.
  ISBN 1-57747-035-4
  1. Gettysburg Campaign, 1863. 2. United States—History—Civil War,
1861-1865—Cavalry operations. 3. Pennsylvania—History—Civil War,
1861-1865—Cavalry operations. I. Title
E475.51 .W58   973.7349   LCC 98-84529

Printed and bound in the United States of America

Published by THOMAS PUBLICATIONS
              P.O. Box 3031
              Gettysburg, Pa. 17325

Cover design by Ryan C. Stouch

Cover illustration "Medal of Honor," courtesy of Don Stivers

Dedication

This book is respectfully dedicated to the memory of all those men, both Blue and Gray, who served in the cavalry, who heard the bugles call "Charge," and who suffered and died for causes in which they believed, including a bold and fearless rider, Brig. Gen. Elon J. Farnsworth. It is also dedicated to my loving and patient wife, Susan Skilken Wittenberg, without whose support this project never would have been possible.

Photo Credits

Photograph of Oliver Cushman on page 38 is from the Gil Barrett Collection, USAMHI, Carlisle, PA. The photo of William Wells on page 41 is from the Wilbur Collection, University of Vermont Library, Burlington, VT. The photo of Adna Chaffee on page 84 courtesy of Kenneth Lawrence, D.D.S., Youngstown, OH. All other period photographs are courtesy USAMHI, Carlisle, PA.

A Bold and Fearless Rider

A bold and fearless rider
A leader tried and true
As e'er amid the storm of war
The brand of battle drew.

Where coward souls might falter
Or fools be rashly vain
He never rashly drew his steel
Or weakly drew his rein.

—From the diary of Silas D. Wesson, 8th Illinois Cavalry, entry for July 5, 1863. *Civil War Times Illustrated* Collection, United States Army Military History Institute, Carlisle, Pennsylvania.

All I ask of fate is that I may be killed leading a cavalry charge.

—Major General J. E. B. Stuart

Those who face the dizzying heights
and cross the dangerous defiles,
who can shoot at a gallop as if in flight,
who are in the vanguard when advancing
and in the rearguard when withdrawing,
are called cavalry generals.

—Zhuge Liang (A.D. 180-234),
The Way of the General.

Table of Contents

Foreword

The clash of infantry at Gettysburg has generally attracted the greatest attention in the study of the Battle of Gettysburg. As author Eric Wittenberg points out, every student of Gettysburg knows of Longstreet's Assault on July 3. The cavalry, except for the now legendary delaying action carried out by Union General John Buford, or the heroics of George Custer in the July 3 cavalry battle, has largely been relegated to the sidelines, as if the role it played in the great clash of armies was less important or significant. While it is true that the cavalry was no longer the shock troop it had once been during the age of the smoothbore musket, it continued to play a critical role in the age of the rifled musket. Its most difficult duty generally occurred before and after the clash of infantry, when it served as the principal means by which an army commander maintained contact with the enemy, secured information about its movements, and harassed or delayed its forces. Maintaining contact with the enemy and gathering vital information was dangerous work with constant risk of getting shot. While the infantry endured a few days of bloody combat during the Gettysburg Campaign, the cavalry was engaged almost daily. Buford's Division, for instance, suffered only 127 casualties during the entire day of fighting on July 1—light losses for that bloody day. Yet, in the period between Stoneman's raid during the Chancellorsville Campaign, to the skirmish at Falling Waters at the conclusion of the Gettysburg Campaign, the division lost 1,813 men, a testament to the constant combat in which it had been engaged.

On the third day of the Battle of Gettysburg, cavalry was engaged on both flanks of the two armies. The large cavalry action three miles east of Gettysburg between Confederate General J. E. B. Stuart and Union General David M. Gregg is relatively well known by Gettysburg students. The other action, involving men of Union Brigadier General Elon Farnsworth's Brigade and Brigadier General Wesley Merritt's Brigade, is less known. "Farnsworth's Charge," as it came to be called, was a part of this action. It is an event of some note in the battle, but is generally discussed or examined as a separate action, out of context with the operation as a whole. The ill-fated attack of Farnsworth's Brigade was actually an element of what Union cavalry commander General Alfred Pleasonton intended to be an attack by both Farnsworth and Merritt against the exposed right and rear of Lee's army. Drawing from a wide variety of sources, Eric Wittenberg tells this interesting and dramatic part of the July 3 battle at Gettysburg in detail, placing it in context with the rest of the battle so that it finally may be understood.

D. Scott Hartwig,
Gettysburg, Pennsylvania

Acknowledgments

I have studied Union cavalry activities in the Gettysburg Campaign for years. Thus, I knew of a number of major cavalry actions on the afternoon of July 3, 1863, including Farnsworth's Charge, Wesley Merritt's fight on the South Cavalry Field, and the debacle at Fairfield. I wanted to learn more about these little-known actions, but discovered that there simply is not much quality material available. I realized that these significant engagements deserved a detailed study. Consequently, I decided to tackle the project. It took several years to gather this material, and the task proved much more difficult than I originally imagined.

All interpretations are exclusively mine, and I accept responsibility for them. I hope the reader finds these three obscure fights as interesting as I do, and that the book will spur new interest in these largely neglected aspects of the Battle of Gettysburg. That is my true motivation for writing; the "what-ifs" of these engagements are just as interesting as the actual fighting. I hope that I have portrayed some sense of that within this book.

In the years that I have studied the Civil War, I have been fortunate to cross paths with some outstanding people. Several have become my mentors. Three individuals have been unquestioningly generous with their time, resources and willingness to help. Each has contributed greatly to my efforts, and each deserves recognition. Clark B. "Bud" Hall, Robert F. O'Neill, Jr., and Brian C. Pohanka, all accomplished historians in their own right, have been extremely helpful, providing guidance and support. Brian and Bob were kind enough to read this manuscript and to provide me with the benefit of their comments. Bud offered invaluable insight, and encouragement to tell the stories of these largely forgotten cavalry actions. These three gentlemen are dedicated to preserving the memory of the men who served in the Civil War. Without their assistance and encouragement, I would not have accomplished whatever I may have accomplished in this field. I am deeply grateful.

I am indebted to: Michael Phipps, licensed battlefield guide at Gettysburg, for the many hours he walked these fields with me and for his useful feedback on my manuscript; Charlie Tarbox, proprietor of the Battlefield Bed & Breakfast and owner of a portion of the South Cavalry Field battlefield, for showing me the more obscure portions of that action; Dave Shultz for providing information on Graham's Battery; and my good friend, touring companion, and business partner, Michael D. VanHuss, who tramped over fields with me and acted as the sounding board for many of my ideas. William R. Howard, Jr. also toured these battlefields with me and gave me the benefit of his opinions.

D. Scott Hartwig, National Park Service historian, allowed me to use the park's resources and also wrote the foreword for the book. Louise Arnold-Friend, Dr. Richard Sommers, and David Keough of the United States Army Military History Institute in Carlisle, Pennsylvania provided invaluable assistance with the project research. Dr. Richard A. Sauers planted the idea for this book in my head, shared his monumental index to the *National Tribune* with me, saved me countless bleary-eyed hours in front of microfilm readers digging for material, and read this manuscript for me. Dr. Elliott W. Hoffman of Rhode Island provided a great deal of useful material on the 1st Vermont Cavalry, including a copy of the proceedings associated with the dedication of the monument to Maj. William Wells on the Gettysburg battlefield. Dr. Kenneth Lawrence provided material on the Battle of Fairfield, as well as some photographs. Colonel Wayne Wachsmuth, a licensed battlefield guide, obtained some additional material and reviewed my manuscript for accuracy. Melody Callahan, who faithfully reenacts the 6th U. S. Cavalry, provided me with several good letters by Lt. Louis H. Carpenter on the Battle of Fairfield.

Thanks also go to Ted Alexander, Dr. Dennis Lawrence, Dave Powell, Terry Johnston, James G. Ryan, David F. and Anita J. Wieck, Dr. Edward Longacre, Dr. Ernie Butner, and Dr. Thomas Desjardin for their time and effort to read this manuscript, and for analysis and criticism of my work. John Heiser did a fine job of preparing the maps. I am grateful to James and Dean Thomas of Thomas Publications for their patience during the writing of this work, and also to Sarah Rodgers, my editor, for her patience and valuable ideas.

Most importantly, I want to thank my wonderful and most understanding wife, Susan Skilken Wittenberg. Without her love and unfailing support, none of this would have been possible.

Eric J. Wittenberg
Columbus, Ohio

Introduction

Most Americans have heard of Pickett's Charge. Many know that the great Confederate assault of July 3, 1863, was the climax of the bloody Battle of Gettysburg. It is commonly believed that Pickett's Charge was the high water mark of the Confederacy and that its hopes for independence were dashed on the rocks of the low stone wall fronting the Angle. The conventional wisdom is that the battle ended with the repulse of the grand Confederate assault and Pickett's retreat across the bloody and broken fields lining both sides of the Emmitsburg Road. This version of history has been immortalized over the course of several generations and perpetuated by the great American producer of pop icons, Hollywood. Most recently, the feature film *Gettysburg* ends with Robert E. Lee's misery as he watches the shattered ranks of his proud army straggle back to Seminary Ridge after failing to take the copse of trees which today marks the High Water Mark of the Confederacy.

Few, however, know that a division-sized Union counterattack, supported by twelve pieces of rifled artillery formed in two batteries, was launched in the wake of the repulse of the grand Confederate assault. Fewer still know that a dashing young commander of a Federal cavalry brigade was killed in action while leading his troopers in a mounted charge that extended more than two miles into the Confederate lines. Only a handful knows that, for a brief moment, Robert E. Lee's Army of Northern Virginia had its flank turned by a daring Federal assault, and that Lee's reeling army could have been driven from the field in a panicked rout. Finally, virtually nobody knows of a bitter but short-lived mounted struggle between forces of Federal and Southern cavalry that took place late in the afternoon of July 3, eight miles behind the Confederate lines, near the small village of Fairfield, Pennsylvania.

These stories have languished untold for a number of reasons. One reason is that it is far more romantic to think that the great, sanguinary Battle of Gettysburg ended with the repulse of Pickett's Charge. Literary treatments of the battle, such as the now legendary *The Killer Angels* and its progeny, the film *Gettysburg*, focus on the romantic side of the grand assault and portray the repulse of Pickett's men as the end of the battle. Because the unsuccessful Union counterattack was made by only two unsupported brigades of cavalry, it is not romantic to remember it. It is not in keeping with the romance of Pickett's Charge for people to believe that the Union launched a counterattack in the wake of Lee's repulse.

Another reason is that the National Park Service has done little to encourage the memory of these actions. Although the Civil War veterans were responsible for the erection of monuments on the battlefield, the Park Service has failed to place any meaningful interpretation on these neglected portions of the great battlefield at Gettysburg. For example, nearly every Federal general officer killed at Gettysburg has a monument to his heroic death, but Brigadier General Elon J. Farnsworth, the slain Union cavalry leader, does not. There is only one monument to the charge, to Major William Wells of the 1st Vermont Cavalry, who rode with his commander, Farnsworth. There are no wayside markers to commemorate either Farnsworth's Charge, or Brigadier General Wesley Merritt's stubborn fight along the Union left flank that afternoon. Only the handsome statue of Wells visibly commemorates either phase of the fighting and is the sole monument to Farnsworth's gallant charge. Indeed, the South Cavalry Field, isolated to the south of the Round Tops, is devoid of interpretation and is probably the least visited portion of the vast battlefield. The monument to the 5th U. S. Cavalry, of Merritt's Brigade, is possibly the single least visited site. It is no stretch of the imagination to say that only a handful of people make the difficult trek through the brambles to the site of that lonely monument each year. Another cavalry fight took place eight miles away at Fairfield, a site which gets virtually no visitation. Only a dilapidated War Department marker and a small plaque erected by the veterans of the 6th U. S. Cavalry along the Fairfield-Orrtanna Road (now known as the Carroll's Tract Road) provide evidence that a battle was ever fought there. Yet, two Federal troopers were awarded the Medal of Honor for their heroic performances there.

In recent years, these largely forgotten cavalry fights have received some well-deserved attention from historians, but no book has told fully the story of these three interconnected but distinct actions. For example, the book which is considered the definitive work on the role of cavalry during the Gettysburg Campaign devotes precisely one page to Merritt's fight. The lack of detailed coverage is remarkable. Given the vast number of books written about Gettysburg, someone should have paid appropriate tribute to these forgotten actions. More than 130 years after the end of the battle, this book attempts to do so. It sets the stage for these climactic fights, introduces the key players in these dramas, and describes the tactical aspects of the three actions. It also examines the controversial question of whether Elon Farnsworth was killed in battle or committed suicide to escape the pain of his severe wounds. Analysis of these fights as they were, and what they could have been, follows. This study concludes by examining the reasons why these fights have been so ignored by historians for generations and suggests changes that can be made to bring more attention to these neglected aspects of the Battle of Gettysburg.

The reader will cross paths with such familiar figures as Confederate Lt. Gen. James Longstreet, Brig. Gens. Evander Law and Jerome Robertson, and Col. William C. Oates, of the 15th Alabama Infantry. Familiar Union figures are Maj. Gen. Alfred Pleasonton, the commander of the Federal Cavalry Corps, and Brig. Gens. John Buford, Wesley Merritt, George Armstrong Custer, and Judson Kilpatrick. The terrain covered by these fights traverses such familiar sites as Little Round Top, Big Round Top, the Plum Run Valley (Valley of Death), and the Emmitsburg Road. The heroism of individual soldiers is related, including the Medal of Honor exploits of Maj. William Wells of the 1st Vermont Cavalry and Sgts. Martin Schwenck and George C. Platt of the 6th U. S. Cavalry. The tragic and heroic death of Elon Farnsworth is explored in detail. Wherever practical, the words of the participants are used to tell the stories.

Perhaps the reader will gain an appreciation for these forgotten cavalry actions by the end of this book. What is more important, the reader will have an appreciation for the opportunities lost late in the afternoon on July 3, 1863. Perhaps only George McClellan at Antietam had a better chance to deal Robert E. Lee a death blow. For just a moment, total victory, perhaps the end of the war, was in the grasp of the Army of the Potomac. For many reasons, some valid and some not, the Federal high command let that opportunity slip away. It did not present itself again until the final days of the war in the spring of 1865. While the death of the brave young Farnsworth was a tragedy, the continuation of the war for nearly two more years as a result of this lost opportunity is perhaps the greatest tragedy of the Battle of Gettysburg.

Chapter

1

"We will stay and fight it out...."

The Strategic Situation on the Afternoon of July 3, 1863

The Union Army of the Potomac and the Confederate Army of Northern Virginia spent July 1 and 2, 1863 locked in mortal combat. The second day was brutal—the two armies suffered combined casualties of more than 16,000 men, with heavier casualties on the Federal than on the Rebel side.[1] The fighting continued late into the night before it finally sputtered out. At the end of the day, the Army of the Potomac held a shorter, fishhook-shaped line anchored on high ground. The prominent points on this line were Culp's Hill and Cemetery Hill on the northern end, and Little Round Top and Big Round Top on the southern end. Between these hills ran a low ridge called Cemetery Ridge. Maj. Gen. George G. Meade's Army of the Potomac had the advantage of holding the shorter lines anchored on good ground. But Meade was not convinced that his army should stand and fight at Gettysburg. He preferred a formidable defensive line in Maryland, along the banks of Big Pipe Creek.

Around 9:00 p.m. on July 2, Meade convened a council of war. He called together his two wing commanders, his seven corps commanders, his chief engineer, and his chief of staff. The Federal brass debated the merits of staying and fighting at Gettysburg versus retreating to the Pipe Creek line for some time, until Meade finally put it to a vote. Polling his generals, Meade found that the majority favored staying and fighting at Gettysburg. Accordingly, he resolved to "stay and fight it out."[2] He had strong forces available to stay and fight despite two days of battering. Almost an entire infantry corps, the Sixth, was fresh; only one of its divisions had been engaged in the fighting on the second.

Meade knew that Confederate commander General Robert E. Lee would resume the attack in the morning. The only question was where.

Lee had tested both of the Union flanks on the second and had failed. Reasoning that Meade had shifted troops to his flanks to meet threats, Lee concluded that the Federal center would be weakened, and he resolved to attack it with the corps of Lt. Gen. James Longstreet the next day. Longstreet's veterans would have to attack uphill across an open field a mile wide, hitting strongly defended Federal positions atop the commanding high ground. It would be a difficult task at best. The attack would be preceded by a great artillery barrage intended to knock the potent Federal artillery out of commission, to clear the way for the grand infantry assault.

Lee's army lay on an extended line, curving at both ends and roughly parallel to the Federal position. His position was several miles long and did not have the advantage of the interior lines. To support his grand attack properly on July 3, and because of the heavy losses his army had suffered on July 2, Lee had somewhat weakened his flanks. In particular, he had largely stripped his right to support the infantry assault on the Federal center, and only a small force of battered infantry was available to hold the flank, which was vulnerable to being turned. As dawn broke on the morning of July 3, Lee's army faced a difficult task.

Previously, as Longstreet prepared to launch his sledgehammer blow on the exposed Federal left on the morning of July 2, Brig. Gen. John Buford's two tired and battered brigades of Federal cavalry rode off the battlefield at Gettysburg, ordered to Maryland to guard the Army of the Potomac's wagon trains, then near Taneytown. Buford's departure left no Federal cavalry on the southern part of the battlefield, and only Brig. Gen. David M. Gregg's depleted division was near the battlefield, pinned down and battling Confederate infantry of the legendary Stonewall Brigade on Brinkerhoff's Ridge, approximately two miles east of the main battlefield on the Hanover Road. This meant that there was no cavalry force available to screen the Federal left flank and no good force available to gather intelligence about the Southern dispositions on the morning of July 3. This would prove critical in the coming fight.

Brigadier General Wesley Merritt and his Regulars

On the morning of July 1, Buford faced Lt. Gen. A. P. Hill's Corps with only two-thirds of his force. To his great regret, one of his brigades, the Reserve, or Regular, Brigade, commanded by Brig. Gen. Wesley Merritt, had been detached to patrol the passes through the South Mountain range in Maryland, several days before the beginning of the battle. The Reserve Brigade consisted of some of the best cavalrymen in any army of the Civil War. It had a nucleus of the four regiments of Regular Army cavalry attached to the Army of the Potomac, along with a fine volunteer regiment, the 6th Pennsylvania Cavalry, so it was no wonder that Buford regretted losing this fine brigade on July 1.

The four Regular Army regiments were the 1st, 2nd, 5th, and 6th U.S., the latter a

Brig. Gen. Wesley Merritt.

new regiment formed at the beginning of the war. These Regular units had been improperly used during the early phases of the Civil War and were largely understrength by the Battle of Gettysburg. The 6th Pennsylvania Cavalry had done so well at the Battle of Brandy Station that Buford told Cavalry Corps commander Maj. Gen. Alfred Pleasonton, "These men did splendidly yesterday; I call them now the Seventh Regulars."[3] In fact, some Confederates believed that the Lancers were Regulars; when George W. Watson of the 12th Virginia Cavalry wrote his memoirs of the Civil War many years later, he called them the Seventh Pennsylvania Regulars.[4]

The men of the Reserve Brigade were proud, well-disciplined professionals who had borne the brunt of the 14-hour fight at Brandy Station on June 9, 1863, and a day of severe fighting at Upperville, Virginia on June 21. By the time of the Battle of Gettysburg, the Reserve Brigade numbered 52 officers and 1,870 enlisted men.[5] They were supported by Capt. William H. Graham's Battery K, 1st U. S. Artillery, consisting of six three-inch rifles, organized into three sections of two guns each.

The Regulars were commanded by 29-year-old Wesley Merritt, a West Pointer, who graduated twenty-second out of 41 members of the Class of 1860.[6] He was assigned to the Second Dragoons and served in John Buford's company at Camp Floyd, Utah. After the outbreak of the Civil War, he came east with the Second Dragoons, now known as the 2nd U. S. Cavalry, and served as aide-de-camp to Brig. Gen. Philip

St. George Cooke, commander of the Army of the Potomac's cavalry forces and father-in-law of Confederate cavalry chieftain Maj. Gen. J. E. B. Stuart. Cooke was known as the father of the U. S. cavalry and wrote the official manual for cavalry field operations. He was an outstanding role model for the young West Pointer. Merritt performed ably as Cooke's aide, and he later served as ordnance officer under the Army of the Potomac's first Cavalry Corps commander, Maj. Gen. George Stoneman. When Alfred Pleasonton was promoted to command of the Cavalry Corps after the Chancellorsville Campaign, Merritt assumed active command of the 2nd U.S.[7]

At the Battle of Brandy Station, Merritt performed conspicuously and caught Pleasonton's eye for his courage and leadership skills. Merritt again distinguished himself at the Battle of Upperville on June 21, and, as a result, Pleasonton requested Merritt's promotion to brigadier general. Pleasonton had been disappointed with the performance of the two officers who commanded the Army of the Potomac's brigade of Regular Cavalry after John Buford was promoted to division command. The first, Major Charles J. Whiting, was relieved of command of the Reserve Brigade for allegedly treasonous conduct following Brandy Station.[8] Whiting's successor, Maj.Samuel H. Starr, performed badly at Upperville. One member of the 6th U. S. Cavalry wrote of the Battle of Upperville:

> The men were pretty thoroughly disgusted with the affair of [the Battle of Upperville]. Major Starr, to whose want of judgment and feeble efforts on this occasion the defeats were proudly chargeable, took an early opportunity to deliver the regiment a lecture, in the presence of the Second Cavalry, in which he charged the Sixth with cowardice during the first part of the conflict. Of course, this was resented, and, in a less-disciplined body of men, might have led to difficulties.[9]

After Upperville, Pleasonton knew that Starr was not competent to command a brigade and realized that the morale of the men would suffer under him. Recognizing a void and knowing Merritt was the man for the job, Pleasonton wrote:

> It is necessary that I have a good commander for the regular brigade of cavalry, and I earnestly recommend Capt. Wesley Merritt to be made a brigadier-general for that purpose. He has all of the qualifications for it, and has distinguished himself by his gallantry and daring. Give me good commanders, and I will give you good results.[10]

Pleasonton had high expectations of Wesley Merritt based on his prior performances.

By the time of the Battle of Gettysburg, Merritt "was a pleasant, handsome young fellow, wearing his rank with easy grace, and apparently possessing just the temperament for a cavalryman."[11] He was considered a protege of his former company commander John Buford, and was of the same mettle. Quiet, modest, tough, and competent, Merritt possessed tremendous personal courage and leadership skills. Another old dragoon described Merritt as "tall, slender, and intellectual-looking. He had a constitution of iron, and under a rather passive demeanor, concealed a fiery ambition."[12] Although clean-shaven and baby-faced, he was known as a martinet.[13] One officer of the 6th Michigan Cavalry said of him, "Modesty which fitted him like a garment, charming manners, the demeanor of a gentleman, cool but fearless bearing in action were his distinguishing characteristics."[14] Bvt. Brig. Gen. Theophilus F. Rodenbough, who served under Merritt in the 2nd U. S. Cavalry, made the following observations:

> Merritt at his high prime was the embodiment of force. He was one of those rare men whose faculties are sharpened and whose view is cleared on the battlefield. His decisions were delivered with the rapidity of thought and were as clear is if they had been studied for weeks. He always said that he never found that his first judgment gained by time and reflection. In him a fiery soul was held in thrall to will. Never disturbed by doubt, or moved by fear, neither circumspect nor rash, he never missed an opportunity or made a mistake.[15]

Merritt was not infallible, as these observations by a member of the 3rd Indiana Cavalry demonstrate: "[Merritt] hails from West Point, girt with the usual amount of red tape and slight show of military capacity. Mind may at length triumph over matter, but thus far humbugs win the race between wisdom and ignorance."[16] As shall be seen, he made serious errors on July 3 that cost good soldiers their lives.

Years later, Merritt wrote memoirs of his service in the Civil War. Describing the twelve-day period between Upperville and the last day of the Battle of Gettysburg, he wrote:

> ...while the history of these days is disposed of in a few sentences, it must not be imagined that the work was not severe. Every day and many nights we marched and countermarched, through good weather and bad, over mountains and through woods, subsisting as best we could on the army ration, when it was possible to obtain it, or "living on the country," which in that district—filled as it was, with soldiers who were hungry and citizens who were naturally trying to save for their own uncertain future— was a precarious living at best.[17]

Another officer of Buford's Division observed:

> The cavalry...had been in active service for nearly a month; men and horses had about reached the limit of endurance; intense heat and dust, hard fighting, short of food for men and forage for horses, had done its work; hundreds of horses had fallen unable to rise again; officers and men tramped on foot, leading their horses to save the little strength left in them....[18]

In part because of the heavy pounding it received in the early phases of the Gettysburg Campaign, the Reserve Brigade was detached on June 29, and sent to Mechanicstown, Maryland (today, known as Thurmont, near Camp David), where it spent two days picketing, scouting, and patrolling the roads and mountain passes in order to protect the Army of the Potomac's lines of retreat and communications. Buford was unhappy about losing his favorite brigade for the critical assignment he faced on July 1. On June 30, Buford requested on several occasions that the Reserve Brigade be sent to him.[19] The request was not granted, and Buford was forced to make do with only two of his three brigades.

On July 2, the Reserve Brigade was finally relieved of its duty guarding the wagon trains and marched to Emmitsburg, Maryland, only eight miles from the Gettysburg battlefield. It spent the day patrolling and picketing through the mountains.[20] The Regulars camped at Emmitsburg on the night of the 2nd and received orders to come to the battlefield on the morning of the 3rd.[21]

On the night of July 2, a squadron of the 1st U. S. Cavalry, commanded by Capt. Isaac R. Dunkelberger, picketed a road, looking for Confederate cavalry. Dunkelberger, a Pennsylvanian, posted some 20 men in advance of a fork in the road. He set up other vidette posts manned by at least six or eight men. He then spent the night visiting the various vidette posts. He recalled, "On visiting my largest and most important post I found to my surprise and horror, every man lying on the ground dead drunk. I replaced the pickets with other men, packed the drunken men back on horses, placed them under arrest and put a guard over them, and expected to prefer charges with a view of setting a terrible example of their misconduct." Before he could do so, however, orders to march to Gettysburg came through, and the court-martial charges were quickly forgotten—all of the men of the command would be needed.[22]

By that time, Buford's other two brigades were in Westminster, Maryland, guarding the Army of the Potomac's wagon trains. After being heavily engaged all day on July 1, Buford's two brigades were withdrawn from Gettysburg on Pleasonton's orders and sent to guard the army's lines of communications and supply at the critical rail head at Westminster, duty which would allow Buford an opportunity to rest and refit his worn-out command.[23] Merritt's Brigade was therefore unattached to any command when it marched to Gettysburg. Early on the morning of July 3, the Reserve Brigade began moving toward Gettysburg via the Emmitsburg Road. They arrived in the Gettysburg area around 11:00 a.m. Upon their arrival, the Reserve Brigade, minus the 6th U. S. Cavalry, which was temporarily attached to Cavalry Corps headquarters, was assigned to Kilpatrick's command for the rest of the battle.

A Hell of a Damned Fool:
Brigadier General Judson Kilpatrick

The only other Union cavalry command on the main battlefield at Gettysburg was one brigade from the Third Division of Brigadier General Hugh Judson Kilpatrick. Kilpatrick, a 27-year-old West Pointer, was a year behind Merritt at the academy, but got his general's star earlier. Ever vigilant for opportunities for self-promotion, Kilpatrick realized that the fastest route for advancement lay in the volunteer service. With the assistance of Lt. Col. Gouverneur K. Warren, one of Kilpatrick's instructors at West Point and a future hero of the Battle of Gettysburg, Kilpatrick obtained a volunteer's commission. He became captain of Company H of the 5th New York Infantry, also known as Duryee's Zouaves, and was the first Regular Army officer wounded in the Civil War when he was shot during the 1861 Battle of Big Bethel. He returned to duty later that year as lieutenant colonel of the 2nd New York Cavalry and served well during the campaigns of 1862. By December 1862, he was colonel of the regiment. Two months later he achieved brigade command and obtained his brigadier's star on June 14, partly as a reward for fine service during the Battle of Brandy Station.[24]

Kilpatrick, known by the unflattering moniker "Kill-Cavalry" for his penchant for using up his command's horses, had a somewhat unsavory reputation. Personally brave, he was known as a vainglorious womanizer. With a reputation as "flamboyant, reckless, tempestuous, and even licentious,"[25] Kilpatrick was one of the most controversial soldiers in the Army of the Potomac.[26] It was also known that he held grandiose dreams, even seeing himself elected president of the United States. He was one of those scalawags that men either loved or hated; with Judson Kilpatrick, there was little middle ground.

Captain Willard Glazier, of the 2nd New York Cavalry, clearly idolized Kilpatrick:

> He is certainly an orator as well as a warrior. He speaks too, as he fights, with dash and daring. What he has to say he says with such perspicuity that no one doubts his meaning...Strict as he is to enforce discipline, and thorough, yet he is not severe; and the men love him for his personal attention to their wants, and for his appreciation of their labors. If he gives us hard work to do in march or line of battle, he endures or shares with us the hardship.... His plans are quickly made and executed while all possible contingencies seem to have been foreseen....[27]

Not all saw Kilpatrick in such a favorable light. Captain Charles Francis Adams, of the 1st Massachusetts Cavalry, descendant of two United States presidents and possessed of an acid pen, wrote, "Kilpatrick is a brave, injudicious boy, much given to blowing and will surely come to grief."[28] Another Federal officer called Kilpatrick "a frothy braggart without brains."[29]

In 1864, Maj.Gen. William T. Sherman said that he "is a hell of a damned fool," but continued, "he's just the sort of fool I want." Lt. Col. Theodore Lyman, who served on Meade's staff in 1864 and 1865, observed that, "it is hard to look at [Kilpatrick] without laughing."[30]

His veteran division consisted of two brigades. One of those brigades, the Michigan Brigade, commanded by Brig. Gen. George A. Custer, was on detached service with two brigades of Brig. Gen. David McM. Gregg's Second Division several miles from the main battlefield near the important road intersection at the junction of the Hanover Road and the Low Dutch Road. Kilpatrick did not learn that Custer's men had been ordered to Gregg until later in the day on July 3.[31] That afternoon, Custer would win fame on what later became known as East Cavalry Field. However, the departure of Custer's Brigade left Kilpatrick without enough troopers to guard the Federal left flank.

Brig. Gen. Judson Kilpatrick.

A Bold and Fearless Rider:
Brigadier General Elon J. Farnsworth and His Brigade

Brig. Gen. Elon Farnsworth.

The other brigade, commanded by Brig. Gen. Elon J. Farnsworth, consisted of approximately 1,200 mostly veteran troopers of the 1st Vermont Cavalry, the 1st West Virginia Cavalry, and the 5th New York Cavalry. The fourth regiment, the 18th Pennsylvania Cavalry, was a green unit. The majority of this brigade, however, had served as a cohesive unit since the campaigns in the Shenandoah Valley during the spring and summer of 1862 under the command of Brig. Gen. John Hatch. It then served under Buford during the Second Bull Run Campaign. These troopers had served well and earned the respect of their commanders and their enemies. However, the brigade was lightly armed, not all of the men having received carbines.[32] It was supported by Battery E, 4th U.S. Artillery, consisting of four three-inch rifles, and commanded by Lt. Samuel S. Elder.

Since June 28, the brigade had been commanded by 25-year-old Elon J. Farnsworth. The young brigadier was born on July 30, 1837, in the small hamlet of Green Oak, Michigan. Descended from veterans of the French and Indian War, the Revolutionary War, and the War of 1812, Elon Farnsworth came from a family of patriotic, hard-fighting men.[33] He was the nephew of an influential Illinois congressman, John F. Farnsworth. When Elon was 17, his family relocated to Rockton, Illinois, and at age 18, he enrolled in the University of Michigan.[34] During his sophomore year, the mischievous young man was called on the carpet for leading student hijinks and was nearly expelled. During his third year at the university, he and several of his friends "engaged in a drinking frolic" in which another student died after being thrown out of an upper-story window of a campus building. Farnsworth and the others were expelled.[35]

His academic career over, Farnsworth joined the army's march to the Utah Territory as a civilian foragemaster. He remained at Utah's Camp Floyd until the outbreak of the Civil War. When his uncle John F. Farnsworth organized and armed the 8th Illinois Volunteer Cavalry, young Elon joined the regiment and was quickly commissioned a first lieutenant. He was popular with the men, who believed that his "shrewdness and wit were proverbial."[36] He was "tall, slight, stern and pale" and was "courage incarnate but full of tender regard for his men."[37] Captain James H. Kidd, of the 6th Michgan Cavalry, who had attended the University of Michigan with Farnsworth, recalled that "a more intrepid spirit that he possessed never resided within the breast of man.... He was proud, ambitious, spirited, loyal, brave, true as steel to his country and his convictions of duty, and to his own manhood."[38]

In early 1862, shortly after being promoted to captain, the impulsive Farnsworth heard of a pastor in Alexandria, Virginia, who failed to offer the customary prayer for the health of President Lincoln. The young cavalry officer approached the parson and asked him to recite the usual prayer for the president's health and well being. When the parson refused, Farnsworth demanded that he do so. When he refused again, Farnsworth had him arrested. Several members of the congregation assaulted the young lieutenant, and it took the threat of shooting them to settle the dispute.[39]

The Confederates feared and hated him. In November 1862, after J. E. B. Stuart's raid into Pennsylvania, members of the 8th Illinois Cavalry encountered elements of the 1st Virginia Cavalry near Warrenton, Virginia. In a brief skirmish, a Confederate trooper named Billy Dulin had his horse shot out from under him, and was pinned under the beast. Farnsworth drew his pistol and shot the trapped trooper, mortally wounding him. The men of the 1st Virginia Cavalry swore vengeance on Farnsworth, and every man of Dulin's company "had his [Farnsworth's] name engraved upon their cartridge boxes, and that it would be only a matter of time until he would meet his fate."[40]

Late in 1862, just after the Dulin episode, Farnsworth became seriously ill and was unable to serve in the field for a time.[41] After he returned and performed further good service with the 8th Illinois, Brig. Gen. Alfred Pleasonton selected Elon Farnsworth to serve on his staff during the spring 1863 campaigns. He appears to have done well in that capacity. Farnsworth caught Pleasonton's eye at Brandy Station, when casualties among the 8th Illinois' officers left him the senior officer in the regiment, and he returned to the regiment to assume command for the afternoon phase of the battle.

Pleasonton was known as a toady, and he regularly courted the favor of his political patron, John F. Farnsworth, now an influential Congressman who still held the rank of brigadier general. Perhaps in an effort to curry favor with the elder Farnsworth, Pleasonton wrote on June 23, "Captain Farnsworth has done splendidly—I have serious thoughts of having him made a brigadier general.... I am sadly in want of officers with the proper dash to command cavalry—having lost so many good ones—Do assist us until we can get ahead of the Rebs."[42] The young captain was not above using political influence to promote his career. In a letter to his uncle written on June 29, he wrote:

...The general speaks of recommending me for Brig. I do not know that I ought to mention it for fear that you will call me an aspiring youth. I am satisfied to serve through this war in the line in my regt as a Capt on Genl Pleasonton's staff. But if I can do any good anywhere else of course "small favors &c." Now try and take this into the President, and you can do an immeasurable good.[43]

This tactic was successful. Along with Merritt and Custer, Elon Farnsworth was promoted from captain to brigadier general of volunteers on June 28 and took command of a cavalry brigade under Kilpatrick.

Maj. Gen. Alfred Pleasonton.

He did not have long to wait before an opportunity to prove himself in command presented itself. On the morning of June 30, Kilpatrick ran into J. E. B. Stuart's cavalry in the town of Hanover, Pennsylvania, 24 miles from Gettysburg. There, a nearly day-long battle raged in the streets of the town, with Farnsworth leading the decisive charge that drove the Confederates out of the town. Two days later, Kilpatrick and Stuart tangled again at Hunterstown, Pennsylvania, where Farnsworth joined Custer and his brigade in attacking the brigade of Confederate Brig. Gen. Wade Hampton. A few of his troopers may have reached Gettysburg late in the afternoon of July 2 in time to assist in the repulse of the Confederate assault on Little Round Top.[44] In the short time he wore a general's star, Elon Farnsworth proved to be an inspirational leader of men who was not afraid to lead charges. This trait would soon cost him his life.

Around 8:00 a.m. on July 3, Kilpatrick's troopers were camped a few miles from the battlefield, near the hamlet of Two Taverns, Pennsylvania. That morning, Pleasonton issued orders to Kilpatrick to attack the Confederates with all of his available cavalry forces.[45] Pleasonton instructed Kilpatrick to "move to the left of our line and attack the enemy's right and rear with [your] whole command and the Regular Brigade," which was on its way to the sound of the guns and which would arrive around 11:00 that morning.[46] Shortly after receiving those orders,

Kilpatrick went looking for Custer's missing brigade. Lieutenant Eli Holden, of Kilpatrick's staff, overheard Farnsworth tell Kilpatrick, "I think you should reprimand Custer severely," to which the division commander replied, "I hope it may not be necessary."[47] Several hours later, the whereabouts of Custer's Brigade was reported, and Kilpatrick learned that Custer had been assigned to serve with Gregg. Farnsworth's Brigade came onto the field at about 10:00 that morning. His troopers briefly halted behind Big Round Top, then crossed Marsh Creek, and moved up behind the main Union line of battle.[48]

In obedience to Pleasonton's orders and still hoping that Custer would soon arrive, Kilpatrick told Farnsworth, "Put your brigade in and commence fighting till Custer comes up. I will post the artillery [Elder's Battery]."[49] Major John Hammond of the 5th New York Cavalry noted that the position taken by Farnsworth's Brigade was posted "near the old road, crossing Upper Plum Run and Little Round Top.... It is a fact that we were inside of a portion of the Fifteenth Alabama's line of battle unbeknownst to ourselves...we were placed on the same line as the infantry, on Little Round Top, and not at a right angle with our main army." The position taken by Farnsworth's men was "in the edge of an open oak forest...Plum Run at the foot of the side of the declivity. The J. Slyder house and the Emmitsburg Road in full view."[50]

Kilpatrick and Farnsworth had established their headquarters near Elder's guns.[51] The young brigade commander sent forward skirmishers from the 1st Vermont Cavalry, which found the Confederate rear near the Bushman farm, and spent much of the day pinned down by Confederate infantry from the brigades of Brig. Gens. Evander M. Law and Jerome Robertson, whose fire took a toll on Farnsworth's command. Farnsworth sent out one scouting party, which followed Plum Run toward the Slyder farm buildings. There, they "ran into a force much too strong for them, turned to the right, and came in by the old road at a lively gait, with quite a number of rebels who were getting the sabre over their heads to quicken their steps."[52]

The Confederate Forces Facing Merritt and Kilpatrick on July 3, 1863

Facing Farnsworth were some of the finest infantrymen available to Lt. Gen. James Longstreet. Longstreet had stripped the right flank of his First Corps position to launch and support the grand assault now known as Pickett's Charge. Only the badly depleted division of Maj.

Gen. John Bell Hood, now commanded by Brig. Gen. Evander M. Law, guarded his flank. Law, a 27-year-old South Carolinian, and a graduate of The Citadel,[53] had distinguished himself in many of the Army of Northern Virginia's battles and normally commanded a brigade in Hood's Division. Hood had been seriously wounded during the fierce fighting on July 2, and Law, the ranking brigadier, assumed command of the division. Law was "one of the handsomest of men, as straight as an arrow, with jet black beard, and of dashing ap-

Brig. Gen. Evander Law.

pearance. The grace of his manner was flawless."[54] He was also a solid and dependable commander who could be relied upon to perform competently under fire.[55] His division had taken extremely heavy casualties in its efforts to capture Little Round Top and Devil's Den. It consisted of four brigades: Law's Alabamians, Brig. Gen. Jerome Robertson's Texans, Brig. Gen. Henry Benning's Georgians, and Brig. Gen. George T. Anderson's Georgians.

Law's Brigade consisted entirely of Alabama troops, including the 4th, 15th, 44th, 47th, and 48th Alabama regiments. These five regiments had spent the afternoon of July 2 locked in mortal combat with infantry of the Federal Fifth and Third Corps, vying for possession of the critical high ground of Little Round Top. In the process, the brigade suffered heavy casualties. One of Law's regiments, Col. William C. Oates' 15th Alabama Infantry, had been hammered during its monumental struggle with Col. Joshua L. Chamberlain's 20th Maine infantry regiment, which had held the far left flank of the Army of the Potomac. After a protracted and bloody struggle, the tired and battered Alabamians fell back and assumed a line which bent to the south around the base of Big Round Top.

Thirty-nine-year-old Brig. Gen. George "Tige" Anderson led the other Confederate infantry brigade, which would be most heavily engaged with Kilpatrick's cavalry on the afternoon of July 3. The Georgian's brigade held the Confederate far right flank, with some assistance from the 1st Texas of Robertson's Brigade. Anderson's Brigade consisted of the 7th, 8th, 9th, 11th, and 59th Georgia. This brigade sustained heavy losses in the brutal battle for the Wheatfield on July 2, and was down about a third from its original strength of approximately 1,800 men. Anderson had been severely wounded in the fight, struck in the thigh by a Union ball. Command of the brigade devolved upon Lt. Col. William Luffman of the 11th Georgia.[56] As Anderson's Brigade went into battle on July 3, it also had at its disposal approximately 100 troopers of the 1st South Carolina Cavalry, under the command of Col. John L. Black, and several batteries of artillery. Black brought his cavalry up and "into a small field of the finest Timothy I ever saw. It was very thick & 3 feet high."[57]

One of those batteries actually belonged to Maj. Gen. J. E. B. Stuart's Cavalry Division. Capt. James Hart's South Carolina horse artillery had been battered at the hands of Union horse artillery at the Battle of Upperville. "Every piece but one" of Hart's Battery "was disabled, two were dismounted, and borne off on caissons.... Hart's Battery did not accompany the movement of the cavalry, owing to its disabled condition."[58] One of the guns was dismounted when its limber chest was struck by a direct hit from a Union artillery shell, causing Hart to leave one of his prized Blakely guns behind.[59] After quickly-performed major repairs to the remaining guns, two guns of Hart's Battery traveled with the main body of the Army of Northern Virginia and were placed to support the Confederate right flank on July 3.[60] Arriving on the right of Law's position, Hart's Battery moved past a woodlot, past the Kern Farm and into an open field, near "a large gate on the southeastern slope of the hill beyond the house."[61]

In addition to Hart's Battery, the Confederates had two other batteries, Capt. William K. Bachmann's Palmetto (South Carolina) Light Artillery, consisting of four Napoleons, and Capt. James Reilly's Rowan (North Carolina) Artillery, consisting of two ten-pounder Parrott rifled guns, two Napoleons, and two three-inch ordnance rifles. Both were veteran artillery units. Bachmann's Battery was largely made up of German immigrants from Charleston, South Carolina, and had been in service since the fall of 1861. It had fought in each of the Army of Northern Virginia's major engagements and "was well known in the army and enjoyed a fine reputation. It is due to the men who composed it to say that, like their comrades of the Confederate army, they bore their hardships and did their duty without flinching."[62] The Rowan Artillery was also a veteran unit, well suited to support the Confederate right flank.

Thus, the Confederates could bring twelve pieces of artillery to bear on this portion of the field. These batteries did not participate in the support of Pickett's Charge. All of the Confederate forces, including their artillery, were concentrated around the A. Kern Farm, located at the intersection of Ridge Road and the Emmitsburg Road.[63]

Merritt's men reached the field at around 11:00 a.m., and he sent out skirmishers to engage the Confederates. These skirmishers remained in position throughout the great cannonade that preceded Longstreet's assault on the Union center and held their positions as the attack was repulsed and the battered Confederates fell back. The regimental historian of the 6th Pennsylvania Cavalry of the Reserve Brigade described his vantage point for the grand charge:

> A brisk skirmish was kept up until about 1 o'clock in the afternoon, when the enemy suddenly opened with heavy fire of artillery, and pressed forward upon the left of our line. First one great gun spoke; and then, as though it had been the signal for the commencement of an artillery conversation, the whole hundred and twenty or more opened their mouths at once, and poured out their thunder. A perfect storm of shot, shell, and ball, rained upon and about us. Every possible shelter was gained behind barricade and stone wall, while the movements of the enemy were carefully watched, and every ordinary advance promptly checked. Our own batteries were splendidly served in reply to the enemy, while the earth trembled beneath the unearthly roar and tumult. The air seemed full of fragments of bursting shell and ball while the sounds peculiar to the several projectiles told of the determination of the attack. There was the heavy whoo! whoo!—who-oo! of the round shot. The "which-one? which one?" of the fiendish Whitworth gun, the demoniac shriek of "what-you-doing-here?" of the shells, and the buzzing Minie, all combined to give it the character of high carnival of powers infernal.[64]

The Federal troopers rode out the storm, and watched in awe as the butternut wave crashed against the blueclad shore behind the stone wall at the Angle.

At around 3:30 p.m., the last stragglers of Longstreet's great assault fell back to their original lines along Seminary Ridge. Colonel William C. Oates of the 15th Alabama Infantry recalled that the Army of Northern Virginia's "confidence in the skill of their commander remained unshaken, although he had ordered them to perform an impossibility—they had been repulsed and were torn and bleeding."[65] Against this backdrop, the stage was set for the two-pronged counterattack now known as Farnsworth's Charge and the battle for the South Cavalry Field. Eight miles behind the Confederate lines, at the small town of Fairfield, another drama was getting ready to play out, one which would also have great impact on the outcome of the campaign and the war.

Brig. Gen. William E. "Grumble" Jones and His Confederate Cavalry Brigade

Brig. Gen. William E. "Grumble" Jones.

As Lee's army advanced toward its date with destiny in Pennsylvania, one of its best cavalry brigades—that of 39-year-old Brig. Gen. William Edmonson "Grumble" Jones—was assigned the task of bringing up the Confederate rear. Grumble Jones had earned his nickname—he was irascible and prone to complaining. However, the Confederate cavalry chieftain, J. E. B. Stuart, respected him. Although he greatly disliked Grumble Jones, Stuart nevertheless called him "the best outpost officer in the army."[66] Stuart also praised Jones' "marked courage and determination," indicating a grudging respect for Jones' abilities.[67] At the same time, however, when Jones was promoted to brigade command in October 1862, Stuart resisted the promotion, writing to his wife Flora, "...I hope he will be assigned to the Infantry, I don't want him in the Cavalry, and have made a formal statement to that effect."[68] Returning Stuart's disdain, Jones referred to Stuart as "that young whippersnapper."[69]

After graduating from Emory and Henry College in Virginia in 1844, Jones matriculated at West Point. Graduating twelfth out of 48 in the Class 1848 (which included John Buford), Jones spent his entire Regulas Army career in the mounted arm, serving on the frontier in the Regiment of Mounted Rifles until his resignation in 1857. He spent much of his career fighting Indians and serving garrison duty in the Pacific Northwest. After leaving the Army, he spent the next several years as a reclusive farmer, living a lonely and bitter life.

He had not always been so short-tempered. His young wife was washed from his arms in a shipwreck shortly after their marriage, and

Jones never recovered from her loss. He grew "embittered, complaining and suspicious" as a result, quarreling with his fellow officers frequently.[70] Eschewing the flamboyant style of dress and the exaggerated mannerisms adopted by Stuart, he was a plain dresser with a legendary talent for profanity. Jones was an extremely strict disciplinarian whose men respected but did not love him.[71] While not a likeable man, Grumble Jones was definitely a fighter. His fellow cavalry general, Brig. Gen. John D. Imboden, wrote that Jones "was an old army officer, brave as a lion and had seen much service, and was known as a hard fighter. He was a man, however, of high temper, morose and fretful.... He held the fighting qualities of the enemy in great contempt, and never would admit the possibility of defeat where the odds against him were not much over two to one."[72]

At the outbreak of the Civil War, Jones formed a cavalry company and was elected its captain, serving under J.E.B. Stuart in the First Manassas Campaign. He became colonel of the 1st and later the 7th Virginia Cavalry and was promoted to brigadier general on September 19, 1862. Shortly thereafter, Jones assumed command of the veteran cavalry brigade formerly commanded by the legendary Brig. Gen. Turner Ashby, one of the best brigades of cavalry in either army. Ashby, a gifted horseman and leader, formerly commanded the 7th Virginia. Promoted to command of Thomas J. "Stonewall" Jackson's cavalry during the 1862 Shenandoah Valley Campaign, Ashby performed well during the campaign until he was killed in action in June 1862. In his short tenure as a commander, Ashby left his mark on his brigade. Proud and dashing, Ashby embodied the attitude of the *beau sabreur*.[73] The brigade Jones inherited consisted entirely of Virginians, the 6th, 7th, 11th, and 12th Virginia Cavalry Regiments and the 35th Battalion of Virginia Cavalry, all veteran troopers accustomed to hard marching and hard fighting.

Jones' men did splendidly at Brandy Station, where, badly outnumbered by the division of his West Point classmate John Buford, they held their own in a day of intense fighting.[74] As the Gettysburg Campaign commenced, Jones' men held the critical gaps in the mountain ranges on either side of the Shenandoah Valley on the march north, and screened the Army of Northern Virginia's rear guard during the advance into Pennsylvania. As the 3-day battle began at Gettysburg, Jones' Brigade crossed the Potomac River at Williamsport, Maryland, and camped near Greencastle, Pennsylvania.[75] Two units of the brigade were left behind as the rest of the brigade advanced north. The 12th Virginia remained in the lower Valley to watch the Federal troops garrisoned at Harpers

Ferry, and the 35th Battalion was temporarily attached to the Confederate cavalry brigade of Brig. Gen. Albert G. Jenkins in the Confederate advance to the Susquehanna River. The balance of Jones' troopers remained behind the Confederate lines, guarding the trains during the first two days of the battle.

On July 3, Jones' Brigade reached Cashtown, five miles from the Confederate line along Seminary Ridge, and halted for breakfast. Later that morning, as plans for Pickett's Charge were being prepared, a note arrived from Robert E. Lee requesting "a force of cavalry to be sent at once to the vicinity of Fairfield, to form a line to the right of and rear of our line of battle."[76] Jones ordered his men "to horse" at 1:00 p.m., and the column of Confederate troopers spread across the Pennsylvania countryside between Cashtown and Fairfield. With Jones in the lead, the 7th Virginia, under command of Lt. Col. Thomas C. Marshall, and the 6th Virginia, under the command of Maj. C. E. Fluornoy, followed. Captain Roger Preston Chew's Battery of horse artillery and Col. Lunsford Lomax's 11th Virginia brought up the rear.

As the Confederate artillerists scrambled to get ready for the tremendous cannonade which preceded Pickett's grand assault, Jones' men continued their march toward Fairfield. The town itself had little strategic significance, but the two passes at Jack's Mountain, Fairfield Gap and Monterey Pass did. If Jones could take and hold the gap, Lee's shortest line of retreat toward the Potomac River would be protected. It was, therefore, critical that Jones get to Fairfield and hold the gaps. Along the way, the Rebel troopers encountered shaken teamsters from a Confederate supply train, who reported the presence of Yankee troopers in the area.

As the brigade left Cashtown, the guns of the artillery barrage preceding Pickett's attack opened. About three miles into the march, Gunner George Neese of Chew's Battery described the spectacle from a high hill near the small village of Orrtanna:

> At one point...we saw nothing but a vast bank of thick battle smoke, with thousands of shells exploding above the surface of the white, smoking sea. Our line looked to me from our point of observation to be about three miles long and enveloped in thick smoke, from which there came a fearful roar and clash of musketry accompanied with a deep continuous roll of booming artillery, such as an American soldier never heard before on this continent. The artillery fire at one time was so heavy that the hills shook and the air trembled, and the deep thunder rolled through the sky in one incessant roar like as if giants of war were hurling thunderbolts at each other....[77]

As the Confederate assault petered out and the survivors staggered back toward safety on Seminary Ridge, the Union high command prepared to launch a division-sized counterattack and the drama at Fairfield unfolded. The time was approximately 5:00 p.m.

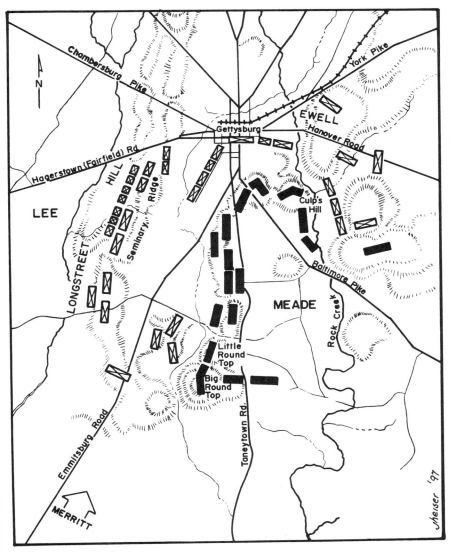

The situation on the afternoon of July 3, 1863.

Chapter

2

"General, if you order the charge, I will lead it, but you must take responsibility...."

Farnsworth's Charge

As the survivors of the grand Confederate charge limped back toward Lee's main line along Seminary Ridge, Judson Kilpatrick saw an opportunity for glory. Under orders from Pleasonton to press the enemy and to attack him at every opportunity, Kilpatrick believed that the battered grayclads were ripe for a counterattack. He was just the man to order it. As the regimental historian of the 5th New York Cavalry described it:

> About 3 p.m., during the most terrific cannonade ever known upon this continent, a large force of Rebel infantry was seen advancing with the evident intention of sweeping away the cavalry, and of then turning our position on Little Round Top, occupied by our artillery with infantry support. To defeat this design of the Rebel chief, became Kilpatrick's animating theme.[1]

Elon Farnsworth's Brigade was the only force available, as Merritt's Regulars were skirmishing along the Emmitsburg Road. Farnsworth's troopers awaited orders in a strip of woods between Ridge Road and Big Round Top.[2] In the meantime, Elder's gunners fired a shot to locate the Confederates. A counter-battery duel erupted, as artillerists from both sides tried to disable each other's guns.[3] The 5th New York Cavalry was dispatched to support Elder's guns and spent the afternoon there, effectively out of the fight. The 5th New York suffered only six casualties that afternoon.[4]

Spotting the 1st Texas Infantry of Robertson's Brigade deployed along the Slyder farm road behind a "very large rock fence,"[5] Kilpatrick decided to attack with Farnsworth's Brigade. Battered the day before in the fight for Little Round Top, the 1st Texas could muster only 196 officers and men for duty on July 3 and were badly under strength.[6] They were supported by two batteries of artillery and held a strong defensive position. If the charge were successful, Farnsworth could break the Confederate line of battle and give Meade's infantry the opportunity to strike the decisive blow of the war. Perhaps the White House would await Judson Kilpatrick after all, if he could only pull off his scheme. Colonel Nathaniel P. Richmond's 1st West Virginia was sent forward to make an attack that seemed foolhardy to the waiting Rebels—one later described by the Yankee troopers as seemingly executed in "a state of intoxication."[7]

The West Virginians drew sabers, charged, and immediately ran into a sturdy rail fence that proved to be a formidable obstacle. The desperate Mountaineers attempted "to throw [down] the rails, tugging at the stakes, cutting with their sabers, and failing in the vain effort."[8] Thomas L. McCarty of Company L, 1st Texas, recalled that he and his comrades spotted the Yankee charge forming and deployed to meet it:

> We had scarcely finished [deploying], when the Federal cavalry...charged. We formed behind a Bunch of Timber in our front between it and us, being an open field for Two Hundred Yards. The ground trembled as they came, they rode down our skirmishers and charged us, and in a few seconds were on us, our Boys arose and pitched into them, they went right through us cutting right and left. In a few minutes great numbers of riderless horses were galloping around, and others with riders on were trying to surrender, a fusillade of shot and shell from Riley's Battery passed a couple of feet above our heads....[9]

The West Virginians crashed into the Texans, and a wild melee broke out, peppered by bursts of canister from the Southern guns. H. W. Berryman of Company I, 1st Texas, noted, "As I was in front [as a skirmisher], cavalry came very near running me over, but I jumped behind a stone fence and held my position."[10] Another of the Rebels recorded:

> Our first impression was that we were hardly equal to the task of successfully resisting such vastly superior numbers, but the men of Hood's Brigade never did learn to retreat; so, as we had a stone fence of about three and a half feet high in our front, our decision was to hold our position, give them a reception, and take the risk of being overpowered and captured.[11]

The Texans waited until the charging Federals were within 50 or 60 yards of the stone wall before opening fire. Their carefully aimed shots

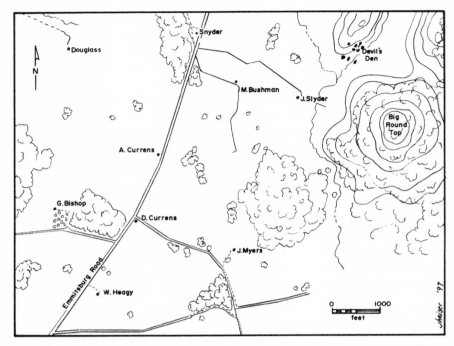

The area of Farnsworth's charge and the "South Cavalry Field."

took down many horses and riders and broke up the momentum of the charge.[12] Because most of the Texans had no opportunity to reload, many fought the mounted Yankees with clubbed muskets. A Rebel named Moore evidently killed one of the West Virginians with a rock.[13] During the chaos, one of Riley's gunners knocked two unfortunate Mountaineers from their saddles with his rammer.[14] Another gunner later told a member of the 4th Alabama that they had "...a hot time defending their guns."[15]

Surprised by the effective resistance, the Federals reeled back. Captain William Porter Wilkin of the 1st West Virginia noted:

> I had seen many battles, many that were called desperate—and they were; but I never saw anything to compare with the third day's fight at Gettysburg. Our regiment suffered terribly. We were ordered against a brigade of infantry and a battery of artillery in position behind a stone wall. We did charge, and took many prisoners; but it cost us a fearful price. Adjutant Knowles was shot dead by my side. Many others, officers and men, were killed....[16]

The battered Mountaineers retreated and began to regroup. And as the West Virginians reformed, the 18th Pennsylvania waited for orders. Kilpatrick, seeing an entire regiment standing idle, snarled at the regiment's commander: "Why in hell and damnation don't you move those troops out?"[17] The green Pennsylvanians quickly obeyed their orders and charged "without any hesitation" at the wall of flame coming from behind the stone wall.[18] Pouring through the heavy woods and scattered boulders in front of the wall, they came up "to the very muzzles of the rifles of the Confederate infantry," who opened fire on them. Captain William C. Potter recalled that, "The Rebs... seemed to come out of the ground like bees and they gave us such a rattling fire we all gave way and retreated toward the woods."[19] Fortunately, the Rebel volley was too high, and many of the Pennsylvanians were spared certain death.[20] The heavy woods and brush shielded their advance somewhat, but they received a very warm reception from the Texans behind the wall, many of whom waited until the Federal horsemen passed, and then crossed over to the other side of the wall in order to keep up their fire.[21]

After suffering casualties from the massed infantry and artillery fire, the 18th Pennsylvania and a small portion of the 5th New York retired, and their men pulled back across the field, now strewn with dead and wounded troopers and horses. The 18th Pennsylvania fell back, dismounted, and formed a skirmish line which connected with that of the 6th Pennsylvania Cavalry of Merritt's Brigade, who were engaged with the Confederates along the Emmitsburg Road. In the span of a few minutes, the 18th Pennsylvania was effectively out of the fight. During this short engagement, the regiment lost 22 men.[22]

As the West Virginians charged, Kilpatrick watched the action and talked animatedly with Farnsworth. The two officers were dismounted and standing near Elder's roaring guns. Captain William C. Potter overheard Kilpatrick suggest that Farnsworth charge Riley's Battery, which occupied an isolated position at the end of the Confederate line of battle and was vulnerable to capture. Farnsworth responded that the Rebel guns, positioned atop a hill, could not be reached by cavalry because of the high stone walls surrounding the position. This discussion lasted for most of the early phase of the fighting by the stone wall.[23] As the first Federal charge bogged down, the conversation heated. Farnsworth saw that charging the position "was worse than folly and certain destruction." The general approached Maj. John Hammond, the commander of the 5th New York Cavalry, and asked Hammond to walk with him to see what

Monument to the 18th Pennsylvania Cavalry, on Bushman's Hill near the stone wall on the Slyder farm lane.

Monument to the 5th New York Cavalry, next to Elder's Battery atop Bushman's Hill.

chance there was for a successful cavalry charge. Hammond described what they saw: "On our side of Plum Run was and is a stone fence, some of it having a few rails on top. On the opposite side of the fence was swampy ground heavily timbered; on the inner side of the run was a range of boulders and rocks that was appalling." Spotting the same obstacles, Farnsworth commented plaintively, "My, God, Hammond, Kil is going to have a cavalry charge. It is too awful to think of—will be but a slaughter of the boys—they have no chance for themselves."[24]

Major John W. Bennett of the 1st Vermont joined the conversation shortly after this exchange. Farnsworth turned to Bennett and asked, "General Kilpatrick thinks that there is a fair chance to make a successful charge. You have been up in front all day, what do you think?"

Before Bennett could answer, Kilpatrick interrupted, exclaiming, "The whole Rebel army is in retreat. I have just heard from the right, and our cavalry there is gobbling them up by the thousand. All we have to do is charge, and the enemy will throw down their arms and surrender."

Surprised, Bennett replied, "Sir, I don't know about the situation on the right, but the enemy in our front are not broken or retreating." Bennett then described the strong nature of the Texans' defensive position and expressed the opinion that any concentrated cavalry charge would be broken up by the heavy woods and boulders in front of the wall. He closed by saying, "General Kilpatrick, in my opinion, no successful charge can be made against the enemy in my front." Kilpatrick snorted with disgust, but said nothing. Instead, Farnsworth and Bennett rode off to reconnoiter the ground. During their ride, Farnsworth looked at Bennett and stated plainly, "Major, I do not see the slightest chance for a successful charge," an assessment Bennett readily accepted.[25]

Seeing Richmond's West Virginians fall back from the stone wall, Kilpatrick ordered Farnsworth to lead another charge on the Confederate position. Angry, Farnsworth retorted, "General, do you mean it? Shall I throw my handful of men over rough ground, through timber, against a brigade of infantry? The 1st Vermont has already been fought half to pieces; these are too good men to kill."

Disgusted, Kilpatrick responded, "Do you refuse to obey my orders? If you are afraid to lead this charge, I will lead it."

Defiantly, Farnsworth rose in his stirrups and cried, "Take that back! I ask no man to lead my troops forward."

After glaring at his young subordinate, Kilpatrick softened. He said, "I did not mean it; forget it."

Following a brief but awkward silence, Farnsworth spoke words that sealed his fate: "General, if you order the charge, I will lead it, but you must take the responsibility."

A few low words were exchanged, and Farnsworth turned away, saying, "I will obey your order."

Nodding, Kilpatrick earnestly replied, "I take the responsibility." Accordingly, the young general "who had never allowed a reflection upon his courage" rode off to prepare. "Shaking hands with his officers and bidding them farewell," Farnsworth, "with great coolness," set about organizing the charge.[26] The Vermonters grimly prepared for the coming charge: "Each man felt, as he tightened his saber belt, that he was summoned to a ride to death."[27]

This heated exchange was loud enough that the men of the 1st Texas could hear it clearly almost 200 yards away.[28] The coming charge would be no surprise, and the Texans scurried to ready themselves. In the interim, Evander Law had begun shifting forces to meet the Federal threat.[29] He realized that the small 1st Texas could not last long in the face of such odds and acted to meet the challenge. Law watched his

Elder's Battery and monument, atop Bushman's Hill. This was Kilpatrick's headquarters during the charge, and the site of the argument with Farnsworth.

troops deploy "with no small degree of anxiety." He knew that it would be a close call whether the reinforcements would arrive before the Federal charge; he later noted that "I had not long to wait" before the charge crashed into his waiting forces.[30]

Law ordered the 9th Georgia Infantry to disengage from Merritt's front and move to the assistance of the 1st Texas. Hearing firing from Farnsworth's front, the Georgians double-quicked to the aid of the Texans and arrived just as the 1st Vermont was forming to charge.[31] Panting from exhaustion and thirst in the hot afternoon sun, the Georgians hurried across the fields for more than half a mile, at the double-quick. By the time they arrived, the Federals were nearly to Bachman's and Reilly's endangered batteries.[32] Captain George Hillyer of the 9th Georgia later recalled that the approaching Vermonters seemed to hesitate when they spotted his approaching battle flag, but continued on anyway. As Hillyer observed, "...it was rarely ever a healthy thing for cavalry to fight Confederate infantry," so their hesitation is understandable.

The Georgians gave a rousing Rebel yell and charged the Yankees in the open field in front of Bachman's guns.[33] Once the Federals got in his front, Hillyer gave the order to fire, and the resulting volley forced them to swing wider than originally planned. Hillyer captured a handsome Morgan bay from a fallen Vermonter. The winded but victorious Georgians fell into line beside the Texans, sheltered by the stone wall.[34]

Federal artillery shells whistled overhead as the Vermonters formed. The regiment was divided into three battalions: the First Battalion was commanded by Capt. Henry C. Parsons; the Second Battalion by the regiment's commanding officer, Lt. Col. Addison W. Preston; and the Third Battalion by Maj. William Wells. Farnsworth chose to ride with Wells.[35] Preston dismounted the Second Battalion behind a stone wall to support the imminent mounted charge.

Wells was the sort of natural soldier that came to prominence in the American Civil War. Born in Waterbury, Vermont, on December 14, 1837, he came from an old English family. His father was a prominent lawyer, businessman, and politician, and young William had a privileged youth. Upon completing his education, Wells joined his father's business as an assistant, but the clarion call of war soon sounded, and along with three of his brothers, he enlisted as a private in Company C of the 1st Vermont Cavalry in September 1861. Within a few weeks, he was commissioned first lieutenant, and by November 1861, he was a captain commanding a company. After good service against Stonewall Jackson during the 1862 Valley Campaign and under John Buford's tutelage in the Second Manassas Campaign, Wells was promoted to major in December 1862 at the young age of 25.

He led the Second Battalion of the 1st Vermont at Hanover on June 30, and helped repulse the Confederates there. At age 26, he was known as one of the best field-grade officers in the Federal cavalry. General Philip H. Sheridan, a hard man to impress, praised Wells by saying, "He was my ideal of a cavalry officer."[36] This day, he would earn the Medal of Honor for his heroism. Observing the Confederate position, Wells remarked that he "had rather charge into Hell than in there."[37]

The bugles sounded and the Vermonters burst from the woods, sabers drawn. Major Bennett recalled, "away into the jaws of death and into the mouth of hell rode that splendid body of brave men."[38] As they burst from the woods, the charging Vermonters "rode down a rough wood road to where it passed across a slight hollow, beyond which were two stone walls lined with Rebel infantry and back of them some distance was their artillery."[39] One Confederate officer noted: "We soon distinguished...the enemy's cheer. Very soon the head of a line of his cavalry...emerged from the wood, galloping, hurrahing and waving their swords as if frantic."[40] They thundered past Richmond's retreating West Virginians, passed a maimed horse, and burst through the enemy skirmish line. Sergeant Horace K. Ide, of Co. D, wrote that, "Our men jumped these walls and then the reapers of death were busy."[41] Bugler Joe Allen of Company I described the charge:

> We rode at full gallop toward the stone wall behind which the Texas regiment was lying. The Texans had ceased firing, and we knew they were waiting to pick us off at closer range. Our men tried to set up a cheer as we rode toward the fence at a furious gallop, but we could not do it: we were so wrought up from expecting the volley at short range.

As Allen and his comrades approached, an impatient Texan fired too soon, drawing the ire of his company commander. When the volley finally came, most of the balls passed over the heads of the charging Yankees. The thick smoke of battle protected them.[42] Farnsworth reined in his horse at the stone wall and stopped to watch the Vermonters clear the impediment before he resumed his wild ride.[43]

As the Union attack streamed forth from the woods, Law and his staff stood by Bachman's Battery, talking to Capt. James Simons, the battery commander. Seeing the threat posed by the charging Yankee cavalry, Law dispatched staff officers to spur up support.[44] He noted that, "It was impossible to use our artillery to any advantage owing to the close quarters of the attacking cavalry with our own men, the leading squadrons forcing their horses up to the very muzzles of the rifles of our infantry."[45] J. O. Bradfield of Company E, 1st Texas recalled that, "Many of the boys did not take time to withdraw the iron ramrods from their guns, but shot ramrod and all into the bunch. Then it was sabers, bayonets, clubbed muskets, and rocks, as no one had time to reload."[46] W. T. White of the 1st Texas proudly wrote, "We regarded that as one of the best fights we put up during the war, and feel that we should have credit for it."[47] Law watched as the Vermonters overlapped the Texans' flank and passed around them into the fields behind them.

The Federals charged wildly across farm fields and low stone walls, past the Slyder farmhouse, and up the narrow dirt farm road. As they did, they came into view of the Yankee troops on Little Round Top. Lieutenant Col. Thomas W. Hyde of the 7th Maine Infantry, standing near the Federal signal station on Little Round Top, heard firing from the area around Devil's Den and spotted the charging troopers. He noted that Farnsworth's men "seemed...to have penetrated quite a distance into the enemy's lines, but as the ground became opener it was hard to see them charging over fences and up to the woods only to be destroyed by the deliberate fire of the Southern rifle."[48]

General Law, observing from near the Confederate batteries, also intently watched the Yankees charge up the road "in gallant style." He recognized the threat to his position and sent a staff officer off to his main position near Little Round Top "with orders to detach the first regiment he should come on to on that line, face it to the rear, and come in a run to throw itself across the path of the cavalry as they charged up Plum Run Valley."[49]

Years later, he recalled that his command was "in hot water" for a few minutes as the Vermonters thundered along.[50] Law grew increasingly worried until he spotted a "ragged Confederate battle-flag fluttering among the trees at the foot of the opposite ridge, and the men with it soon after appeared, running out into the open ground on the farther side of the valley."[51] That battle flag belonged to the 4th Alabama, of Law's own brigade. Its men had spent most of the day resting after their tremendous fight the day before. A courier rushed up with orders for the regiment to come at the double-quick to the right. Although none of the men knew their intended mission or destination, the Alabamians rushed to the front.[52]

As the afternoon sun blazed, Capt. Oliver T. Cushman of the 1st Vermont's First Battalion spotted the awaiting Confederate skirmish line.

The field between Bushman Hill and the Slyder Farm which Farnsworth's cavalry traversed. (Above) Looking northward toward the Slyder farm. (Below) Looking toward Bushman Hill from the Slyder farm lane.

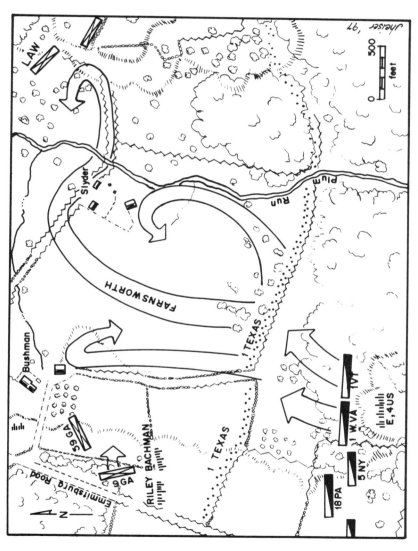

The charge of the 1st Vermont Cavalry and General Farnsworth.

After being battered in the assaults on Little Round Top, the Alabamians had thrown up a line of rock breastworks and assumed a defensive position.[53] Captain James T. Jones, commanding the right of the 4th Alabama, later claimed, "I was ordered to face about to resist cavalry; we marched rapidly to the rear over the rocks and the Vermonters were upon us before we could form. They were within a few paces when we gave the order to fire." Lieutenant Vaughan of Company C loudly ordered, "Cavalry, boys, cavalry! This is no fight, only a frolic, give it to them!"[54]

Rising up, the Alabamians fired a volley that passed over the heads of the Federal horsemen. Private Sam Whitworth of Company F, 4th Alabama raised his rifle to fire at the charging Vermonters. Not seeing his friend Robert Coles immediately to his front, Whitworth struck Coles in the side of the head with his rifle as it fired. Whitworth later apologized for hitting Coles when they laughingly discussed the incident around the campfire.[55] Captain Jones continued, "The whole regiment fired, but when the smoke cleared I only saw one horse fall. A private at my left said, 'Captain, I shot that black.' I said, 'Why didn't you shoot his rider?' He replied, 'Oh, we'll get him anyhow; but I'm a hunter, and for three years I haven't looked at a deer's eye—I couldn't stand it.'"[56]

The surprised infantrymen regrouped and fired a second, ragged volley, which was more effective. Another Vermonter's,

> ...beautiful sorrel mare fell shot in the breast only a few paces from our line. The trooper came down with her, standing erect on his feet, astride of her. Instead of surrendering he quickly threw up his carbine and discharged it directly in our faces, but no harm was done. Then, throwing down his gun, he jumped over his horse and ran. A puff of dust flew out of the blouse which never covered a braver heart, as the bullet penetrated between the shoulders, and he fell, meeting the same fate as his horse.[57]

Bugler Allen of the 1st Vermont recalled that, "Every time a man near me was hit, I could hear the pat of the bullet. I saw several of my companions cringe and start when hit, and a frightened look came into their faces."[58] The Rebel fire forced Parsons' men to take cover along the base of Big Round Top as they reformed. In the meantime, Wells' Battalion swept around to the left in a great circle passing in front of Bushman's Hill and across Parsons' track. Veering across an open valley to the north of the Slyder farm buildings, Wells' column followed a low stone wall up the eastern slope of the spur of Big Round Top known

The Slyder farm buildings. Farnsworth's horse was shot down about 100 yards to the west.

Plum Run located just west of the Slyder farm. This was the position held by the 4th Alabama Infantry.

today as the "one hundred foot hill," coming in behind several regiments of Confederate infantry. Brigadier Gen. Henry L. Benning, commander of a fine brigade of Confederate infantry, saw this action unfold from his vantage point atop Houck's Ridge:

> Some men of ours...threw themselves behind the stone fence on the side of the lane and opened on them as they came down the lane. They then turned again to the right and entered the field and directed themselves back towards the point where they had first appeared to us. In doing so they had to pass a wood on their left. From this an infantry fire opened on them, and their direction was again changed to the right. The result was that they galloped round and round in the large field, finding a fire at every outlet, until most of them were killed or captured.[59]

Wells later wrote that, "We charged over the rocks, over stone walls and fences.... We charged until we ran into a brigade of infantry stationed behind a stone wall in the woods. They opened on us, killed some horses and captured some men."[60] The charge was "swift and resistless...over rocks, through timber, under close enfilading fire."[61] Colonel Preston's Second Battalion joined Wells' column, and the enhanced force headed toward the 100-foot hill, nearly a mile behind the main Confederate skirmish line. Puffs of smoke coming from Rebel muskets provided the only evidence of the Confederate positions.

As Allen rode on, his friend Marv Mason had his horse shot from under him, was thrown over the dying beast's head, and landed on his feet, running all the way back to the main Federal line. Allen also noted that, "Somewhere during the charge, a man rode by me with his leg shot off by a cannon ball. Just above the stump some one had tied the sleeve of a coat, to stop the bleeding. I think seeing this man, with his pale frightened face, is my most distinct recollection of Gettysburg."[62]

At the base of Big Round Top, the column came under fire of Confederate artillery from Bachmann's and Riley's guns, forcing it to split into three parties. One swept west across the open field and fell upon the stunned skirmishers of the 1st Texas, capturing a number of prisoners in the process. The second made a beeline for the Federal lines to the south and east, and made it safely back. The third party, which included Farnsworth, ran into trouble. Farnsworth had his horse shot out from under him, but a dedicated trooper from Company C, David Freeman, gave his horse to the general and escaped on foot. Both Capt. Oliver T. Cushman of the 1st Vermont and Farnsworth turned and tried to escape via their route of approach. W. W. Warner of Company G recalled,

"After breaking the Rebel lines we rode nearly a mile, coming to a peach orchard and an old log barn, where we struck a few skirmishers, who retreated a short distance into the woods."[63] The Vermonters raced back toward the Slyder farm at full speed.[64]

Seeing Farnsworth's predicament, Parsons ordered his squadron to support its comrades. A line of Confederate riflemen appeared on the rocks of a portion of Big Round Top known as the Devil's Kitchen, overlooking the escape route, and opened fire on the trapped Yankee horsemen. As Parsons charged toward Wells' small column, he looked to his left and saw Corporal Ira E. Sperry, who had been riding with him, fall from a Rebel sharpshooter's ball.[65] Parsons and his men wheeled to the left, passing between the Confederate skirmish line and the stone wall behind them, funneling along a narrow line. The Vermonters captured a number of the grayclad skirmishers as they rode past the Alabamians, and some of Parsons' small command turned back toward the Federal lines with their prisoners in tow.[66] Sergeant Horace K. Ide of Company D noted that part of the "body of incomparable infantry that carried the Confederate Government on their Bayonets for four years" threw up the butts of their muskets to signify their surrender.[67]

As the head of the small Federal column cleared the stone wall and passed into open fields behind the Slyder farm, Farnsworth spotted Parsons' men riding to his aid. His silk neckerchief flapping in the breeze as he rode, the young general raised his saber above his head and charged toward the Confederate infantry, which turned out to be the 15th Alabama Infantry of Law's Brigade. Momentarily, the Alabamians were confused by the silk neckerchief, mistaking it for a flag of truce.[68] Then quickly they realized Farnsworth's intentions as the charge thundered toward them. What remained of Wells' Battalion followed him, sabers drawn, cutting their way into the Confederate lines.

The 15th Alabama had borne the brunt of the fighting for the southern end of Little Round Top on July 2, and Col. William C. Oates' command was exhausted. However, Oates received orders to support Reilly's Battery, and he ordered his men forward at the double-quick.[69] The rude surprise of the Federal charge alarmed Oates, who deployed to meet it. The Alabamians wheeled into position at a dead run; the Southern guns belched forth a round of double cannister, which passed just over the heads of the panting infantrymen.[70] Oates threw forward a line of skirmishers, positioned about 30 paces in front of his main line of battle.[71] As they deployed, the mounted Federals crashed into them.[72] Parsons spotted the developing melee and ordered his battalion to join the attack. He wrote, "We charged in the same general direction, but on opposite sides of the wall that runs parallel with the Round Top range, and within two hundred paces of each other."[73]

As Parsons stormed toward the waiting Rebels, he was passed by Sergeant George H. Duncan, "a black-eyed, red-cheeked boy, splendidly mounted, standing in his stirrups," with his saber raised. Flying past, Duncan called back over his shoulder, "I'm with you!," threw up his arm, and fell dead. Parsons' startled horse picked its way over the fallen sergeant, and Parsons was left alone for a moment as the rest of his battalion surged past him. Seeing the lone horseman, Confederate infantry demanded Parsons' surrender. As the intrepid captain raised his saber, a Rebel Enfield pressed against his side and fired, and another wounded his mount, which bolted frantically over the startled grayclads, leapt the stone wall, and scampered down the hill. At the bottom of the hill, the wounded Parsons was met by one of his corporals, who led him safely back to the Union lines.[74] Lieutenant Stephen Clark of Company F noted, "I saw Parsons [hit], saw the men near him, and in my immediate front, in column of fours, melt away before the deadly fire in front."[75]

Clark ordered his company to charge, dashing past Parsons, passing around the 100-foot hill, and directly into a jumble of rocks known as the Devil's Kitchen. Private Loren M. Brigham of Clark's Company F was shot through the head during this charge, "gallantly facing the enemy. His last words were 'Come on boys!'"[76] Surrounded by Confederates, Clark called for their surrender, and, to his surprise, many complied. Faced with the unexpected encumbrance of prisoners, Clark released most of them. Many of the Confederates then escaped to safety behind the stone wall atop the 100-foot hill. Clark ordered his company to come into line in front of the stone wall where they attacked Oates' men with pistols and sabers.[77]

As Clark's company fought Oates' men in front and to the west of the stone wall, Farnsworth's small force arrived, entered a "D" shaped farm field enclosed by high stone walls, and made a dash toward Oates' men, who lay waiting behind the stone wall on the other side of the field. The Alabamians changed front to face Farnsworth's small party. Pistol in hand, Farnsworth demanded the surrender of Lt. John B. Adrian, the officer commanding Oates' skirmish line. Farnsworth raised his pistol, and a dozen Rebel Enfields opened on him, killing his horse and wounding him in several places, including the leg and thigh, the shoulder, and the abdomen.[78] Adrian approached Farnsworth, who still held his pistol and was struggling to stand. Adrian demanded the wounded general's surrender, but Farnsworth refused.[79]

A great deal of controversy exists as to whether Elon Farnsworth shot himself that day. Regardless, the brave general died on the battlefield from numerous serious wounds. The few Vermonters who still rode with him were realistic enough to know that there was no time for them to try to rescue Farnsworth. Frank Doyle of Company M of the 1st Vermont noted, "Owing to the great rush that was made, it would have been madness to attempt to recover his body."[80]

Colonel Oates rested a moment before walking over to the corpse of the fallen Yankee general. One of his skirmishers asked, "Colonel, don't you want this Yankee major's shoulder straps?" and held them up before Oates. The skirmisher assumed that the single star adorning the shoulder straps signified that the officer was a major, because Confederate majors wore a single star on their collars. Oates, however, knew better, and exclaimed, "A Major, the devil! He is a General."[81] Oates approached the body, noticed that it was very bloody, and found a packet of letters in one of the pockets addressed to Gen. E. J. Farnsworth. He

The monument to the 1st Vermont Cavalry, located in the D-shaped field. Farnsworth fell in the vicinity of this monument.

claimed to have read enough of them to know that the letters were from Farnsworth's wife and then destroyed them, to prevent them from falling into the wrong hands.[82] Since Farnsworth never married, this is an interesting observation by Oates.[83] After the war, Oates wrote, "I took from his coat his shoulder-straps, which I still have, and would be pleased to deliver them to his widow if I knew her address."[84] When Farnsworth's body was recovered by the Federals the next day, it had been stripped down to flannel shirt, drawers, and stockings. There were numerous bullet wounds in his body.[85] He was found very near the location of the present-day monument to the 1st Vermont Cavalry.[86]

Some Confederate accounts state that Farnsworth wore an unusual white coat into battle that day. This is not true. Farnsworth, who only learned of his promotion while on the march to Gettysburg, did not have a chance to obtain a general's uniform of his own. He borrowed a blue brigadier general's coat and hat from Alfred Pleasonton and wore them into battle. Captain Oliver Cushman of the 1st Vermont wore the white "fighting jacket" into battle that day, with a silk handkerchief over his cap. Cushman fell at Farnsworth's side, horribly wounded in the face, and was obviously mistaken for the general. Cushman died the next day.[87]

When the Alabamians wheeled to receive Farnsworth's small force, the way was cleared for Lt. Clark's command to escape, and they did so unmolested. After fleeing a short distance, Clark found Maj. Wells and the survivors of the force, which had cut their way through the ranks of the 15th Alabama. Puzzled, Wells inquired, "Clark, where are you going?" Clark pointed at Bachman's Battery, firing away in the distance, and replied, "Gen. Farnsworth is killed, six bullets striking him at once." Wells responded, "We must get out of this," and called out to the rest of his small command, "1st Vermont, rally!" Reformed, the Vermonters rode around the Confederates, going around to the southeast of Little Round Top, and safely

Captain Oliver Cushman.

passed into the lines of the Federal Sixth Corps, positioned in the rear of the Union main line of battle.[88] Clark later noted that, "Maj. Wells had several bullet-holes in his clothes, but was not wounded. I was not hit in any manner, but thought it a most wonderful escape."[89]

The strong position held by Oates' Alabamians probably could not have been carried. It was also the site of the heaviest fighting; Col. Preston of the 1st Vermont reported:

> The contest for possession of this hill was most desperate.... The opposing forces were now completely intermingled, and the contest became a hand-to-hand one, in which our sabers were effectually used. The enemy being completely cut up, surrendered in squads, and were sent to the rear. Had I two companies of carbineers at my command, I think I could have held this position and removed my wounded, but, being exposed to the fire of the enemy's batteries and sharpshooters, I was obliged to fall back... Many of our dead, together with the body of General Farnsworth, were found in the rear of the position held by the enemy's second line.[90]

Upon reaching the safety of the main Federal line of battle, the weary Vermonters learned of the repulse of Pickett's great assault on the Fed-

Monument to Major William Wells of the 1st Vermont Cavalry, on South Confederate Avenue.

eral center. As the men rested, "the heaviest rain I ever experienced was falling; I saw soldiers soundly sleeping that night who were half-covered with running water," as bugler Joe Allen recalled.[91] Corporal George R. Crosby of Company F of the 1st Vermont observed, "It is strange that the whole of Co C was not killed. We had a good many horses killed... ours stood well."[92] For the men of Farnsworth's Brigade, the Battle of Gettysburg was over. The 1st Vermont had suffered heavy casualties in the charge, including 16 men killed or mortally wounded, 16 wounded, and 35 missing.[93]

After the retreat of Farnsworth's Brigade, Capt. Hillyer of the 9th Georgia heard the pitiful cries of a wounded Vermonter. Hillyer noted, "Just in front was a wounded Federal soldier, about twenty steps off. He was suffering intensely with the heat and thirst, and occasionally cried for water. We wanted to relieve him, but it was as much as a man's life was worth to show himself above the wall before the Federal sharpshooters." Calling for a white handkerchief, Hillyer sent a team of litter-bearers to rescue the wounded Federal. As the Georgians crossed the wall, they were spotted by Yankee infantry, posted along the southern end of the main Union line. "Not a shot was fired by them, nor a shot from either side until [the litter bearers] went forward and brought the wounded Vermonter in and laid him down in the shade behind the wall,

The bas-relief of Farnsworth's Charge, on the front of the Wells monument.

*Colonel Addison Preston,
1st Vermont Cavalry,
commanding officer.*

*Major William Wells,
1st Vermont Cavalry.*

*Sergeant Horace K. Ide,
1st Vermont Cavalry.*

*Captain Henry Parsons,
1st Vermont Cavalry.*

where we gave him water and what comfort we could. This day I rejoice more in that act of mercy and kindness than in any other claim of glory or success in the battle."[94]

After the charge was repulsed, some of Law's men ventured from their hiding places to investigate the dead and wounded Yankees surrounding their position. Private Reuben Nix of the 4th Alabama spotted a dead trooper and climbed over a fence to get to the body. Checking the body for identifying marks, he instead found a roll of greenbacks, which he gladly pocketed, a valuable souvenir of a fruitless attack.[95]

Farnsworth's gallant charge "caused the enemy to detach from his main attack on the left of our line," Alfred Pleasonton reported incorrectly.[96] Kilpatrick described the fight:

> At 5:30 p.m., I ordered an attack with both brigades.... Brigadier-General Farnsworth moved down with two regiments—the First West Virginia and Eighteenth Pennsylvania—closely followed by the First Vermont and Fifth New York, through a piece of woods, and drove the enemy from one position to another until a heavy stone wall was reached, behind which the rebel infantry was gathered in great numbers. Our cavalry broke, rallied, and broke again before that formidable barrier, but the First Vermont and First West Virginia, led by the gallant Farnsworth, cleared the fence, sabered the rebels in the rear, rushed on over a second line of infantry, and were only stopped by another fence and a third line of infantry and artillery....[97]

Kilpatrick, who gave the order that cost Elon Farnsworth's life, wrote of his fallen comrade:

> We lost 4 officers killed, 13 wounded, and 4 missing; 34 enlisted men killed, 138 wounded, and 117 missing, making an aggregate of 319 killed, wounded, and missing. In this battle the division lost many brave and gallant officers. Among the list will be found the name of Farnsworth; short but most glorious was his career—a general on June 29, on the 30th he baptized his star in blood, and on July 3, for the honor of his young brigade and the glory of his corps, he gave his life. At the head of his men, at the very muzzles of the enemy's guns, he fell, with many mortal wounds. We can say of him, in the language of another, "Good soldier, faithful friend, great heart, hail and farewell."[98]

Colonel Nathaniel P. Richmond of the 1st West Virginia, who succeeded to brigade command after Farnsworth fell, noted that, "In the death of Brigadier-General Farnsworth this brigade suffered an almost irreparable loss, as a more gallant officer or perfect gentleman cannot, in my opinion, be found."[99]

A few days after the battle, Pleasonton wrote to Gen. John Farnsworth, lamenting the death of his dashing young brigadier:

> My heart is too full to write to you now, all I desire. Your nephew's loss has grieved me far more than I had imagined. In the short time he was with me on the staff, I had learned to love him for very many excellent and devoted qualities. Glorious as was his death, it was a sacrifice too great, too trying for those who knew him—indeed for this Army.[100]

Captain Frederick C. Newhall of the 6th Pennsylvania, serving on Pleasonton's staff, wrote that the order to charge "was a crime" and that he hoped that the gallant cavalryman did not ride "to his death with that contemptible taunt goading him."[101]

The glory of Farnsworth's ride was not lost on the enemy. Years after the war, James Longstreet wrote, "Farnsworth had a rough ride over rocks and stone fences, but bore on in spite of it all, cutting and slashing when he could get at the skirmishers or detachments. He made a gallant ride along the rear of our right, but was obliged to come under the infantry and artillery fire at several points."[102] Captain Felix Robertson, a Texas artillery officer and the son of Brig. Gen. Jerome B. Robertson of the Texas Brigade, later called Farnsworth's Charge an "inexcusable military blunder."[103]

Farnsworth and his small force managed to pierce the Confederate lines and ride for nearly two miles behind their main line of battle. Dr. Ptolemy O. Edson, the regimental surgeon of the 1st Vermont, later told Major Wells that "he never saw such a place for cavalry to charge as that went over by us." Major Charles E. Capehart, who assumed command of the 1st West Virginia after Farnsworth fell, commented in his report of the action:

> I cannot fail to refer you to the defensive position the enemy had availed themselves of, which is one that above all others is the worst for a cavalry charge—that is, behind stone fences so high as to preclude the possibility of gaining the opposite side without dismounting and throwing them down. The whole ground over which we charged was very adverse in every particular, being broken and uneven and covered with rock. Neither can I fail to bring to your notice that this regiment here charged upon infantry, and still did not falter in any of its movements until it had scaled two stone fences and had penetrated some distance the enemy's lines, which had kept up a continual fire of musketry.... Any one not cognizant of the minutiae of this charge upon infantry, under cover of heavy timber and stone fences, will fail to form a just conception of its magnitude.[104]

Wells also observed that "[the] Officers and men [of the 1st Vermont] behaved themselves gallantly."[105] Colonel Preston wrote that, "The charge of Wells' battalion upon a brigade of infantry has seldom been excelled in desperation and valor."[106] Brevet Brig. Gen. Theophilus F. Rodenbough, the leading American cavalry historian of the 19th century, noted that the primary result of the attack was "the moral effect of the charge, the fearless troopers leaping the obstacles and sabering many of the Confederate infantry in their positions."[107] Like the fabled Charge of the Light Brigade, Farnsworth's Charge was brave, memorable, and fruitless.

It is easy to forget that the cavalryman and his mount are a team. Captain Henry C. Parsons of the 1st Vermont praised the animals:

> The behavior of the horses in this action was admirable. Running low and swift, as in a race; in their terror surrendering to their masters, and guiding at the slightest touch on the neck; never refusing a fence or breaking from the column; crowding together and to the front, yet taking or avoiding the obstacles with intelligence, they carried their riders over rocks and fallen timber and fences that the boldest hunter would hardly attempt today; and I doubt if there was a single fall of man or horse, except by shot of the enemy.[108]

Parsons later gave all of the credit for surviving the wound he received at the end of the charge to his faithful horse, which safely brought him back inside the Federal lines despite being wounded itself.[109] If the men of Farnsworth's Brigade suffered, so did their horses. Many were also casualties of the charge. Farnsworth alone had two mounts shot out from under him.

The gallant charge was made by one lone regiment, the 1st Vermont, with support from the West Virginians and the 18th Pennsylvania; the 5th New York Cavalry spent the day standing to horse near Elder's Battery and took little part in the fighting.[110] General Law, who recognized the significance of the Federal threat early in the action, later observed: "Had this force been directed a little to [its] left immediately against our batteries, our position would have [been] a critical one...."[111] However, their attack was misdirected, largely unsupported, and led to no tangible gains. The primary result, it seems, was the death of Elon Farnsworth. A great opportunity was squandered that day, along with Farnsworth's life.

Chapter

3

"He placed his pistol to his own body, shot himself through the heart."

Did Elon Farnsworth Shoot Himself? The Great Controversy

For years, Col. William C. Oates, commander of the 15th Alabama Infantry, steadfastly insisted that Elon Farnsworth shot himself rather than surrender. On March 29, 1876, Oates wrote:

> I received a full discharge of canister from Riley's guns right in my ranks & over our heads. This caused me to halt, which Farnsworth saw, he reined in his hosse [*sic*] & with his pistol in hand ordered Lt. [John B.] Adrian who was in command of the skirmish line to surrender; thereupon Adrian & his line or those near enough fired upon him killing his horse and wounding Farnsworth in several places. He fell. Adrian advanced towards him (his few men never halted) and said "Now you surrender." Gen. Farnsworth replied, "I'll be damned if I do," & placing his pistol to his own head fired & shot his brains out.[1]

Oates repeatedly wrote that he did not witness the event; all that he had to go upon was Lt. Adrian's account.[2] Nevertheless, Oates maintained this version of Farnsworth's death for many years after the war.[3]

Oates retreated from this viewpoint a bit as time passed. On September 22, 1888, he sent a letter to Col. John B. Bachelder, the official historian of the Battle of Gettysburg, which stated:

> Adrian said Farnsworth sat upright on the ground with pistol still in hand as he Adrian advanced and in turn demanded of Farnsworth to surrender and that the latter refused to do it and shot himself.
> I have the impression and always have had, although it may be erroneous that Adrian said Farnsworth shot himself through the head. I did not examine the head, the body and the ground about where it lay being

quite bloody. I noticed two or three bullet holes in different parts of the body from which the blood was issuing.... Lieut. Adrian was subsequently killed in battle and I do not remember the names of the men who were with him on the occasion, hence there is no way at this time of finding a living witness to the occurrence.

Adrian was a faithful young officer and regarded as perfectly reliable and I believe he told the truth, but I could not testify that he said Farnsworth shot himself in the head. I can however and do testify that he said F. shot himself and I do know that a few minutes after when I saw the body he was quite dead.[4]

This account was repeated in a number of publications and created a great deal of controversy over the issue of who could claim credit for mortally wounding Farnsworth and the question of whether or not he shot himself on the battlefield rather than surrender.[5] Given the fact that Oates insisted that he had found letters from the bachelor's wife, his account is rendered somewhat suspect.

George T. Todd of the 1st Texas recounted, "Gen. Farnsworth (believed by us to be Kilpatrick himself) fell in the left front of our regiment, and one of the First Texans ran forward and got his epaulettes and spurs. He also reported that he shot himself on account of the agony he was in."[6] W. T. White of the 1st Texas recorded in a 1922 article for the *Confederate Veteran*:

The general and staff rushed on our boys and demanded their surrender, when one of the boys, by the name of Taylor, and belonging to Company L, of our regiment, shot the general from his horse. As he hit the ground, Taylor said, "Now, —, I reckon you will surrender," whereupon Farnsworth drew his pistol and shot himself.[7]

J. O. Bradfield of the 1st Texas wrote in the same issue:

They came through at the edge of the timber just below the rock fence, General Farnsworth halting at the fence to see his men pass. In passing they cut off Captain Parks and two of his pickets from the regiment. They dodged behind a pile of rocks, but as General Farnsworth turned to go on with his men, he saw them, and, drawing his pistol, ordered them to surrender. Instead of obeying him, one of Parks' men fired, and remarked, "It is your time to surrender now." Farnsworth was shot through the stomach and fell from his horse, but still held to his pistol. He raised to a sitting position and, turning to the man who shot him, said, "I'll be damned if I ever surrender to a rebel!" Then he placed the gun to his head and shot his own brains out. Thus died as gallant a man as ever wore the blue. I was in plain view of the whole scene.[8]

These two accounts are very consistent in their recounting of the story.

Another Texan who claimed to have seen Farnsworth commit suicide was Pvt. A. C. Sims, Co. F of the 1st Texas. Sims wrote:

> If there had been any honor in killing a Federal general, doubtless that honor belongs to the First Texas regiment. It happened this way: Gen. Farnsworth came dashing up to Corporal A. F. Taylor and demanded his surrender, but Taylor replied with a ball from his Enfield, which took effect in his abdomen just below his belt. The general, looking down, saw his wound, turned his pistol on himself, and shot himself four times and fell from his horse, and if those who came to bury the dead were not personally acquainted with him, they never knew they were burying a general.[9]

Sims did not see the climax of the charge, so his knowledge has to be based upon hearsay. Further, the allegation that Farnsworth shot himself four times simply is not credible. An unidentified Texan recounted:

> In his retreat, Gen. Farnsworth came up to where myself and a number of my comrades were concealed in a clump of bushes, when he called out for us to surrender. One member of my company (I have forgotten his name) discharged his gun at the General, shooting him through the hips and unhorsing him. As he fell the soldier called out to Farnsworth, "Now you surrender," when General F. replied, "I will not do it," and drew his pistol and deliberately shot himself through the head, firing three shots, the two first of which went through his hat, the third taking effect and killing him instantly.[10]

It seems unlikely that, badly wounded and surrounded by hostile Confederate infantry, Farnsworth could live long enough to try to shoot himself in the head three different times before finally succeeding. This account lacks credibility.

Captain George Hillyer of the 9th Georgia Infantry related the following account:

> I saw [Sgt. Leslie] Craig coming from the direction of those woods. He walked straight up to me and said: "Captain, those men are Vermont Cavalry, and their commander was General Farnsworth, and he has been killed. I saw him killed. His horse had been shot down and he was on the ground still fighting and firing his pistol. We commanded his surrender, and when we were very close to him he said he would die before he would surrender, and turned his pistol and shot himself." I had learned before from other persons that it was Vermonters we were fighting, but I did not know the name of the commander until Craig told me. Now he told me this certainly within fifteen or twenty minutes from the moment of

Farnsworth's death. I think it likely, however, and I have so heard, that General F. had received several wounds before he shot himself, but Craig did not know it.[11]

It is very unlikely that Hillyer's Georgians were involved in this aspect of the repulse of Farnsworth's Charge, and it is equally unlikely that his men witnessed the actual event of Farnsworth's wounding. A.H. Belo, an officer of the 4th Alabama Infantry of Law's Brigade, put a slightly different spin on the story:

> The Fourth and Fifteenth Alabama were ordered to face about and charge down the lower slopes of Big Round Top to repel [Farnsworth's] cavalry, which we did without difficulty in a few minutes. A volley was fired which killed General Farnsworth's horse and brought him down mortally wounded, and as a squad of Alabamians approached him he pulled a pistol and fired it into his own bosom, killing himself instantly. It is known that Kilpatrick spoke to him offensively, saying that if he [Farnsworth] did not wish to lead it he would lead it himself or find some officer who would, whereupon Farnsworth, with an indignant remark, dashed away at the head of his cavalry, and it has been suggested that the sting of Kilpatrick's remarks may have prompted that final act of suicide. But, as he had five desperate wounds in the breast, it is probably that the agony he suffered from them made him seek immediate death as a relief.[12]

Another member of the 4th Alabama, Robert T. Coles, left the following account:

> I heard that evening two or three versions of how General Farnsworth met his untimely death, and I have been told others since. Lieutenant Adrian of the 44th Alabama, at the time General Farnsworth with his few followers appeared to some of the 4th Alabama to be surrendering, had advanced sufficiently close for General Farnsworth to draw his pistol and order him to surrender. Adrian replied with a volley from his carbine and the rifles of those nearby, unhorsing Farnsworth and two or three of his troopers. The latter, with his pistol still in his hand showed no disposition to surrender. Adrian walked up to him and remarked, "Now you can surrender, sir." Preferring death to captivity, with an oath that he would not surrender, he turned the pistol on his own body and fired, expiring almost instantly. Lieutenant Adrian was one of the best known and most popular of the company officers in the brigade, and was afterwards promoted to a captaincy for his gallantry. This is his version of the affair as he related it to us, and I believe it to be the correct one.[13]

One problem with this account is that Coles had Lt. Adrian armed with a cavalry carbine. As an infantry officer, there was no reason why

Adrian would have been armed with a cavalry trooper's weapon. Henry Benning, who did not see the climax of the charge, reported later:

> Some of the men engaged...told me that in going over the field for spoils they approached a fallen horse with his rider by his side but not dead. They ordered him to surrender. He replied wait a little, or something to that effect, and put his hand to his pistol, drew it and blew his brains out. This was General Farnsworth.[14]

As this account is entirely based on hearsay, it is probably not a reliable account of the death of Farnsworth. A dissenting voice was raised by Capt. William Bachmann, commander of one of the Confederate batteries which contested the charge. In 1910, William M. Graham, who commanded one of the Federal batteries on South Cavalry Field, by then a retired brigadier general in the Regular Army, recorded:

> The following is the account of Farnsworth's death as seen by a Confederate officer and by him related to me in the winter of 1876-77 at Columbia, South Carolina: I was introduced to Captain Bachman, who commanded the "Hampton Legion Battery," with which I was engaged (Battery K, First United States Artillery), at Gettysburg on July 3d. Naturally our conversation drifted to the war, and he remarked: "One of the most gallant incidents of the war witnessed by me was a cavalry charge at the Battle of Gettysburg, on July 3d, made by a General Farnsworth of the Yankee army. He led his brigade, riding well ahead of his men, in a charge against my battery and the infantry supports; we were so filled with admiration of his bravery that we were reluctant to kill him, and so called out to him to 'surrender', as his position was hopeless. He replied by emptying his revolver and then hurling it at us and drawing his saber, when we shot him through the body, killing him. His men were nearly all killed, wounded, or captured, very few escaping to their own lines.[15]

This appears to be the only surviving Confederate account which does not have Farnsworth committing suicide, and it is the only one which has him dying outright from his battle wounds. The Southern accounts were met with immediate, snorting indignity from the Federals who participated in the charge. Dr. Ptolemy O. Edson, the regimental surgeon of the 1st Vermont, left the following account shortly after the battle:

> Early in the afternoon of July 5, 1863, Surgeon Lucius P. Woods, Fifth New York Cavalry, and myself, then Ass't. Surgeon First Vermont Cavalry, found the body of General Farnsworth upon the wooded spur that connects Little Round Top and Round Top at Gettysburg, and carried it to the hospital of the Third Division of the Cavalry Corps. When found, the body was stripped to flannel shirt and drawers and stockings. There were

five bullet wounds upon the body—four in the chest and abdomen, and one high up in the thigh. He had no wound or injury of any sort in the head or face.

In view of these facts it seems improbable at least, that General Farnsworth had any need to shoot himself, though Colonel Oates, who claims to have seen it, was undoubtedly there and has declared that it was suicide. General Farnsworth certainly did not blow his brains out, nor did anyone do it for him.[16]

Many other members of Farnsworth's Brigade rallied around the honor of their fallen commander. Frank Doyle of Company M, 1st Vermont indignantly retorted:

> There are those, I am sure, who know in what manner the General met his death, and I wish for the honor of his family, and those who followed him, that they will come to the front and refute and forever stop this talk of a man killing himself when his body was riddled by bullets, each bullet hole rendering it unnecessary for him to commit suicide...Gen. Farnsworth was not the man to commit suicide. In the first place, he had neither scratch nor sign of wound on the head. On that point we are sure, and have unimpeachable witnesses. Surg. Edson of the 1st Vt. Cav. and Surg. Woods, of the 5th N.Y. Cav., found the body and brought it in. They say there were no wounds on the head whatsoever. There were, however, four or five bullet holes through his chest and abdomen. Now, with all these wounds through the body, each one fatal, it seems impossible that he could have killed himself. Then, had he shot himself through the head and killed himself, how come all those bullet holes through his body?[17]

Captain Henry Parsons noted:

> [Farnsworth] fell with his saber raised, and was found with five wounds in his body, three of them mortal, and with no wound in his head.[18]

The Vermonters, almost to a man, disputed the allegations that Farnsworth had dishonored himself by committing suicide. Lieutenant Eli C. Holden of Company C contended that Farnsworth "died by bullets of the enemy."[19]

Some of the West Virginians and members of the 18th Pennsylvania also rallied around their fallen commander. Captain John Steltzer of Company L of the 1st West Virginia noted that, "We had charged about 400 yards when we came in contact with Hood's Division of rebel troops, whose fire killed Gen. Farnsworth."[20] Major Charles E. Capehart of the 1st West Virginia recorded, "The charge was led by Gen. Farnesworth [*sic*], who fell pierced with five bullets."[21] And Capt. Henry C. Potter of the 18th Pennsylvania wrote that, "In the meantime, Farnsworth was out on the meadow, leading a straggly charging mass of cavalry. He fell at the head of the line near Devil's Den."[22]

It is unlikely that the truth about Elon Farnsworth's death will ever be known. Certainly, there are powerful arguments supporting both sides of the debate. The sheer volume of Confederate accounts contending that he shot himself is impressive. So, too, is their consistent retelling of the story, even though there is disagreement about whether he was initially shot down by men of the 15th Alabama or of the 1st Texas.

On the other hand, the testimony of Drs. Edson and Woods is compelling. Their steadfast insistence that there were no wounds to either Farnsworth's head or face indicates that the accounts which have him shooting himself in the head are untrue. As men of science, these men had little reason to lie. In addition, members of his command, who knew him well, steadfastly insisted that their leader never would have shot himself, regardless of the suffering of his many wounds.

One explanation for the confusion is that Farnsworth was mistaken for Capt. Oliver T. Cushman, who rode with Farnsworth and fell at his side, terribly wounded in the face. Because Cushman was badly wounded in the face, it is altogether possible that the Confederates saw his wounding and confused him for Farnsworth, which would certainly account for the numerous reports that Farnsworth shot himself in the head. The infliction of a bad facial wound could easily be confused with a self-inflicted gunshot to the head during the heat of combat.

Cushman also wore the mysterious "white duck" jacket that many Confederates believed Farnsworth wore into battle that day. Cushman, who was also seriously wounded when Farnsworth fell, fought it out with his pistols until he fainted from the loss of blood. Captain Parsons observed that, "He was a notably handsome officer, and it was clear that he was mistaken throughout the fight for General Farnsworth."[23] For example, Robert T. Coles of the 4th Alabama left an account which indicated that Farnsworth had worn "a long light-colored havelock which we had mistaken for a white flag..."[24] It is clear that at least some members of the 4th Alabama believed that Cushman was Farnsworth.

Whether or not Elon Farnsworth actually shot himself remains open to debate. But there are good reasons to believe that he did not. Farnsworth did not want to make that charge; in fact, he recognized its folly. He led the charge because Judson Kilpatrick challenged his manhood and honor. Farnsworth's contemporary, Capt. James H. Kidd of the 6th Michigan Cavalry, properly noted, "[Farnsworth] was too brave a man and too conscientious to do anything else than obey orders to the letter. His courage had been put to the proof in more than a score of battles."[25] The Civil War was all about honor and duty and devotion. The last full measure of devotion a man could give in that war was to die gloriously in battle, facing the enemy, doing his duty. As modern historian Gerald Linderman wrote:

> Honor...yielded to the centrality of courage but was of a still different quality. Courage...possessed clear definition, but within the meaning of honor—as within duty's—there were broad areas of intangibility, at least to the mind of the twentieth-century observer..., honor [is defined] as "True nobleness of mind; magnanimity; dignified respect for character, springing from probity, principle, or moral rectitude; a distinguishing trait in the character of good men." While courage had to be demonstrated, honor did not.... Courage was the individual's assurance of a favorable outcome in combat.... What...remained implicit—that the courageous would be spared—was made precise...: "I have always believed the most daring came off with fewest wounds." ...There was comfort even for the soldier of courage who might prove himself the exception by being shot down: Those at home would join celebration to their mourning of his death. If the good did die, they died good deaths.... "A brave man dies but once, a coward dies a thousand times."[26]

Elon Farnsworth lived by this code. He was brave and cool in the face of great odds and rode to his death seeking to redeem the honor and courage impugned by Judson Kilpatrick. Redemption came at the fearful cost of his life.

In an era of honor-bound principle, committing suicide was not seen as an honorable or courageous way to die. In particular, suicide in the face of the enemy was an especially inglorious and dishonorable way to die. Suicide in the face of the enemy was neither courageous nor dignified. Rather, the "right" way to die was to go down while still resisting, thereby demonstrating one's honor, courage, and dedication to duty. Because Elon Farnsworth made the charge to defend his honor, it is highly unlikely that he would then commit suicide in the face of the enemy; to do so would dishonor himself, his family, and the brave men who followed him. Thus, it is extremely unlikely that Elon J. Farnsworth committed suicide, Col. Oates' arguments to the contrary notwithstanding.

Chapter 4

"Every one fought like a tiger...."

Merritt's Regulars on South Cavalry Field

As Farnsworth's men began desultory skirmishing around 11:00 a.m., Merritt's Regulars approached the battlefield from the south. They reached the scene shortly after Farnsworth's Brigade began trading shots with the Rebels on the slopes of the 100-foot hill and engaged the grayclad pickets in preliminary and insignificant skirmishing for a couple of hours. One Regular wrote, "the country was so woody & the fences so high that both sides dismounted."[1] Another trooper observed: "It is hilly ground & thickly wooded & at that time a large body of troops might lie very near you & yet not be seen & then positions were being frequently shifted."[2] The Regulars, "soon after crossing a narrow deep creek, came in on the 1st [West] Virginia of Farnsworth's Brigade, this was a narrow country road; we dismounted near a school house, in the woods to the left and moved to the left on foot through the woods...."[3] Merritt's men, with no recent intelligence, had no idea how strong the waiting Confederate force might be. This lack of good intelligence would have severe consequences for Merritt's attacks.

The 6th Pennsylvania men were thrown forward as skirmishers, and their uncontested advance continued for almost a mile. Their regimental historian observed: "The Sixth Pennsylvania, having the advance of our brigade, was the first of the cavalry to become engaged. The men were dismounted, led horses taken to the rear, when we pushed forward to meet the infantry line of the enemy."[4] The advance of the Pennsylvanians was spotted by Col. John L. Black, commanding elements of the 1st South Carolina Cavalry. Black reported this information to Brig.

Gen. Evander M. Law's headquarters and ordered his small command of 100 troopers and the "ragtag and bobtail" of the hospital and wagon trains, a total force of approximately 300 men, to form line of battle. Because he believed that the "ragtag and bobtail" were "a nuisance" and not a "benefit," Black ordered "[t]he part of my command I could rely on dismounted & deployed as skirmishers."[5]

Confederate infantry of Brig. Gen. George "Tige" Anderson's Brigade of Hood's Division held the Confederate far right flank. It suffered heavy casualties on the afternoon of July 2 and was depleted. Four of

Monument to the 6th Pennsylvania Cavalry, located on Emmitsburg Road near the Kern house. This monument is on the skirmish line held by the 6th Pennsylvania, and represents the farthest northward advance by the Reserve Brigade. Note the full scale replicas of the lances on the monument.

its five small regiments—the 8th, 9th, 11th, and the 59th Georgia—had suffered severe losses of both officers and men in the brutal fighting on July 2, while the 7th Georgia had been unengaged.[6] In addition to the infantry, Black's small cavalry force was available, as were the two guns of Hart's Battery and the guns of Riley's and Bachman's Batteries. A significant force of infantry awaited the Federals as they advanced into the fight. The 6th Pennsylvania, according to Capt. Frederick C. Newhall's report,

> ...dismounted and drove them, the carbines and rifles rattling on both sides of the [Emmitsburg] Pike, till the enemy's line was met across the road from Kern's house. It had that confident look of being there to stay, which soldiers appreciate, and either Merritt called a halt, or Law brought him to a stand, just as you may happen to fancy from the report of one or the other.[7]

The stone Kern farmhouse was particularly troublesome to the Yankee troops—it was filled with enemy sharpshooters who took a toll on the advancing Lancers.[8] Finally, supported by artillery fire from Capt. William M. Graham's Battery of horse artillery, which had taken position on the right of the road on a small hill which "had splendid observation of the entire front."[9] Supported by Graham's fire, the Lancers drove the Confederate sharpshooters from the Kern house. Under fire from an entire brigade of infantry and both Riley's and Bachman's Batteries, the Pennsylvanians took shelter behind a low stone wall that ran perpendicular to the Emmitsburg Road, at the site of the present-day monument to the 6th Pennsylvania. Seeing that the Yankee advance was temporarily stymied, Col. Black rode off to the headquarters of Lt. Gen. James Longstreet's Corps to request reinforcements to counter the threat to the Confederate flank.[10]

The position held by the 6th Pennsylvania was about halfway across an open field, which sloped from the woods down to a low point and then back up again to the woods held by the Confederates. Samuel Crockett of the 1st U.S. Cavalry recalled that, "the Pa. Cav. were in an ordinary skirmish line."[11] A portion of the 6th Pennsylvania advanced toward the Kern farmhouse, where it encountered Confederate infantry which "had that confident look of being there to stay."[12] However, the Lancers managed to take the stone house, until Confederate artillery ranged in on the house and drove them from it. The men of the 6th Pennsylvania then fell back to the safety of the stone wall.[13] Captain Newhall later observed:

It is risking little to say that on the whole Confederate line at Gettysburg there was hardly a point so well guarded by the enemy when Merritt's little cavalry brigade, lacking one whole regiment—the Sixth Regulars—and the others reduced by detachments, and the fighting and marching of the last three weeks, came up this way from Emmitsburg....[14]

Not long after the battle, one of Merritt's aides noted: "The 6th Pennsylvania Cavalry was on the advance, and soon found line on, and on either side of the road, and, driving in the enemy's outposts, proceeded untill [sic] within about a mile of Gettysburg where they met the enemy in full force, but still held their own ground."[15]

Two squadrons of the 1st U.S. came into line alongside the Pennsylvanians and added to their fire. Along with a squadron of the 2nd U.S. and a squadron of the 5th U.S., they were assigned to extend Merritt's line and to attempt to outflank Anderson's line. Their position extended to the right of the Lancers in front of Graham's guns.[16] Captain Dunkelberger, commanding Co. E of the 1st U.S., wrote:

A portion of the 6th Pennsylvania Cavalry occupied a stone house in rear of me, the enemy shelled the house, the 6th Cavalry vacated it, and came up on my line. There was a cornfield in my immediate front. The enemy were discovered putting a horse [Hart's] battery in position in my front. I ordered a charge on foot and we captured the battery before they could load but the enemy retook the battery with a regiment of infantry and in retreating I was struck by a spent ball on my left heel.[17]

The men of the 1st U.S. formed a heavy skirmish line and, passing through the dismounted 6th Pennsylvania, struck the Confederate line of battle, driving it back toward its artillery support.[18] Worried about his ability to hold, Black went searching for reinforcements and found two regiments of infantry leisurely marching toward his position. Spotting an officer wearing a colonel's insignia, Black told the commander of one of the regiments, "Damn it all, Colonel, if you don't move faster the enemy will lap before you are in position."

The officer responded, "Oh, no, I think not," and hurried his troops toward the sound of the firing. Black later learned that the "colonel" was Evander Law himself, who, inexplicably, wore the insignia of a colonel. Law ordered his command into line of battle and to open fire on the advancing Yankees.[19] Law later noted that by dismounting and fighting as infantry, Merritt lost his numerical advantage, and Law "lost no time taking advantage of this temporary equality."[20] He detached the 11th and 59th Georgia and sent them around to the right, personally placing the men of the 11th in line of battle.

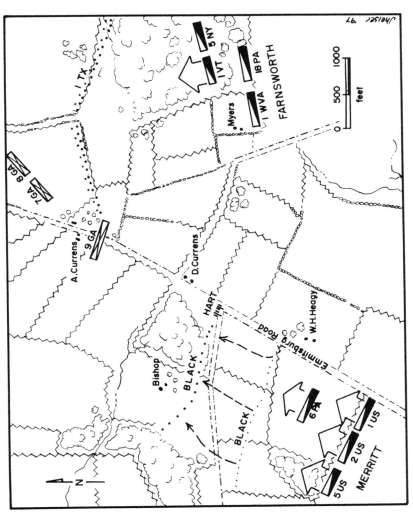

The advance of the 6th Pennsylvania Cavalry and the retreat of Black's skirmish line.

Private Samuel Crockett of the 1st U.S. recalled that, "We soon whipped their cavalry & drove it nearly a mile to their reserves. A whole Regt of Infantry rose up at once in a wheatfield and gave us a volley. We knocked their colors down three times but our little squadron of more than 70 men could not hold their own against so many though every one fought like a tiger."[21] The Confederate artillery fire took a toll on the advancing Regulars, forcing them to halt their advance. Law noted after the battle: "Hart's guns...were well handled, and did good service as long as the enemy remained in reach of them."[22] However, Hart's gunners evidently did not think much of the fight on South Cavalry Field, because a sketch of the battery's history referred to this fight as only "desultory skirmishing," a description which appears understated.[23]

Law ordered the Georgians to strike Merritt's line "on its end and double it up."[24] Captain Dunkelberger noted:

> When we attacked on the right and left of the Emmitsburg Road, we then entered the enemy's right and rear, had we been successful we could have occupied their line of retreat. But the real object of our attack was to force the enemy to draw troops from their main point of attack (Pickett's Charge) and repel us. In this we were successful as the Divisions of Hood and McLaws were held back to repel our attack.[25]

The air was thick with Confederate minie balls, and, as the 1st U. S. pulled back, they were pursued by Black's cavalry. Black later crowed, "We drove them clean away & Law took his Regiments and went back saying he hoped I could hold the ground."[26] The concentrated artillery fire of three Rebel batteries deployed near the woods further encouraged the withdrawal of the Yankee troopers.

In response, Merritt brought Graham's Battery to the front, supported by elements of the 1st and 2nd U. S., and placed it in a position where it could support both his attack and that of Farnsworth's Brigade.[27] Graham's guns were placed on the military crest of a small plateau several hundred yards in front of the position of their present day monument.[28] Counting Elder's guns, about a quarter of a mile away, Merritt could bring 10 rifled pieces into play, balancing the heretofore unequal contest between the dismounted cavalrymen and the Rebel batteries. There, Graham's gunners "poured a stream of shot and shell into the ranks" of the Confederates and into their artillery support.[29] The intense Federal artillery fire drove the Southerners back, forcing them to vacate their strong position at the Kern house.[30] One Regular noted that Graham's guns "inflicted severe punishment on the enemy."[31]

Monument and guns of Graham's Battery on South Cavalry Field.

Captain William M. Graham.

This action left Hart's two guns open to capture. Hart wrote that, "Here a considerable skirmish occurred with the Federal cavalry. Our line was too short, and a Federal column extended across the road by the Kern house, and enveloped our right completely, penetrating some distance to our rear. I was forced to retire to where Bachman and Riley's [sic] batteries were in position."[32] Law keenly observed: "It is not an easy task to operate against cavalry with infantry alone, on an extended line, and in an open country where the former, capable of moving much more rapidly, can choose its points of attack and can elude the blows of its necessarily more tardy adversary."[33] The opening phase of the fight on the South Cavalry Field lasted for more than two hours, as the two sides jockeyed for position. For a short time, Merritt's men had the upper hand in the fight, and things looked bright for the attack of the Regulars.

Around this time, Maj. Gen. George G. Meade, commanding the Army of the Potomac, sent a dispatch to General-in-Chief Henry W. Halleck, which said, "My cavalry are pushing the enemy on both my flanks, and keeping me advised of any effort to outflank me."[34] This language indicates that Meade intended only an action to tie up the Confederate flanks and not to turn them. Thus, it appears that Merritt's attack was doomed to failure from the beginning, as it would be unsupported.

At approximately 5:00 p.m., Farnsworth's grand charge started. By then, Merritt's men had been engaged with the enemy for several hours, in a fight of varying intensity. While Farnsworth met his destiny on the rocky slopes of Bushman's Hill, the Regulars continued fighting to the south and west, hoping to pin down the Rebel infantry and prevent it from being used against Farnsworth's horsemen. When Farnsworth's leaderless brigade eventually fell back, the 18th Pennsylvania connected with the Lancers, and linked the two commands in a solid line of battle.[35]

In conjunction with Farnsworth's charge, Kilpatrick also ordered a supporting attack by the Regulars. Merritt ordered the 5th U. S. to make a mounted charge on the exposed far right end of the Confederate line of battle. The 5th U. S., known as the 2nd U. S. Cavalry before the war, was a crack regiment. It produced a number of prominent officers in the antebellum period, including Albert Sidney Johnston, Robert E. Lee, and 16 other officers who achieved the rank of general in the Civil War. The 5th performed well. At the June 27, 1862, Battle of Gaines's Mill, Brig. Gen. Philip St. George Cooke, then commanding the Regular cavalry, ordered a futile charge by the 5th U. S. in an effort to halt a Confederate breakthrough. The Regulars made a brave but unsuccessful charge, losing all six of the regiment's officers in the process. Wesley Merritt, who was there, later noted that, "...your cavalry and the audacity of its conduct at that time,...did much toward preventing the entire destruction of the Union army at Gaine's Mill."[36] At Brandy Station, the 5th U. S. bore the brunt of the fighting for the Union for a time and carried a stone wall held by dismounted Confederate troopers.[37] They came into the Battle of Gettysburg a proud, veteran unit with an enviable combat record.

At Gettysburg, they were commanded by Capt. Julius W. Mason, a Pennsylvanian who had been commissioned directly and was not a West Pointer. Mason proved to be a competent cavalry commander over the course of the war, receiving two promotions and a brevet prior to Gettysburg.[38] His small command, battered at Brandy Station and still further at Middleburg and Upperville, mounted only 306 officers and men on July 3.[39] One of those officers was 29-year-old Lt. Temple Buford, nephew of the Reserve Brigade's division commander, Brig. Gen. John Buford.[40]

The regimental historian of the 6th Pennsylvania recalled that, "The 5th United States Cavalry made a mounted charge, driving the enemy from an advanced position, and giving us great advantage."[41] The Yankee charge nearly captured Hart's guns, but Law spotted Merritt's approaching attack and took personal command of the situation, rushing infantry support up just in time to save the guns. Captain George Hillyer of the 9th Georgia, whose men had already double-timed across the fields to assist in the repulse of Farnsworth's charge, now brought his command back, finding that

Captain Julius W. Mason commanded the 5th U.S. Cavalry at Gettysburg.

"the enemy was nearly at the battery. Passing through from behind the guns, with a yell, the regiment charged the enemy in the open field, scattering and chasing them away in a moment, killing and wounding a number and capturing several horses."[42] The 7th and 8th Georgia fell into line alongside the men of the 9th, forming a strong line in support of the artillery.[43] Colonel Black recounted:

> A detachment of Federal cavalry made a dash into our lines, came full tilt down the pike in gallant style, and only met grape and canister from Henry's guns. While the [Georgia] regiment springing up poured a murderous fire into their left flank, on their right was a stone wall.[44]

Law recalled:

> General Kilpatrick at once commenced operations by attacking my flanking lines with dismounted skirmishers of Merritt's Brigade, continuing this movement steadily to my right until the line was stretched out to a considerable distance beyond where it crossed the Emmitsburg Road. This stretching process continued until I became fearful that my line beyond that road would soon become so weak that it might easily be broken by a bold cavalry attack. To avoid this I withdrew two regiments from the main line on the slopes of the Round Tops, and leading them rapidly to my extreme right across the Emmitsburg Road, attacked Merritt's reserve, and then, wheeling on the flank of his line, "doubled it back" to that road just beyond Kern's House. Here I left the two regiments engaged in this movement, together with the 9th Georgia Regiment, that had been previously posted there, under the command of Captain George Hillyer, who had done conspicuous service during the battle.[45]

Major Henry D. McDonald, commanding the 11th Georgia, noted:

> The detachment, guided by Brigadier-General Law (commanding Hood's Division) in person, reached the flank just as the enemy's dismounted cavalry had succeeded in turning the same, driving our cavalry force before them. Under the direction of Brigadier-General Law, I ordered a charge with the entire force, which was promptly made. The enemy was repulsed with loss, and driven in confusion several hundred yards to a point far beyond our flank, before endangered...Being ordered...to stop the pursuit, and recall my command to a fence on the extension of the line of the division, I did so, and sent a small force of skirmishers to the front.[46]

Major B. H. Gee of the 59th Georgia bragged that, "...we charged the enemy at about 3 p.m., driving them before us until they were no longer to be found."[47] Merritt's unsupported attack came to an abrupt halt in the face of three regiments of Confederate infantry supported by

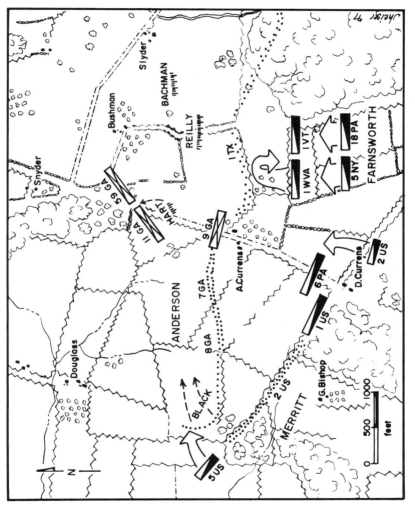

Merritt presses the attack.

three batteries of artillery. Despite this, some of the intrepid Regulars stood and formed a skirmish line to resist the Rebel advance.[48] Law dismissed the charge of the 5th U. S., commenting that their attack "consumed scarcely more time than it takes to write it."[49]

The Southern infantry advanced to silence the Yankee guns, which were taking a toll on both the infantry and the artillery. Private Crockett of the 1st U. S. noted in his diary:

> After waiting behind a stone wall a good while for the rebels to come, Gen. Merritt sent us orders to mount and come to the batteries as the rebel Infantry was advancing in great force. We rode to the batteries and found 20 guns in position in a piece of woods, so placed as to cross fire on a wide open field across which the rebels must advance to attack the guns. We were drawn up in squadrons, some 8 or 10 Regts ready to charge as soon as the artillery had thrown them into confusion. Our dismounted men were steadily firing on them all the time. Three Brigades of rebels came in sight, but none charged the battery.[50]

Major Henry McDaniel of the 11th Georgia wrote:

> The enemy finding our pursuit stayed, made a demonstration against the skirmishers in front. Captain Cockrell was ordered to advance with his skirmishers. This advance was handsomely made, under a sharp fire, and the enemy quickly put to flight. No further attempt was made to penetrate our rear in that direction. Our loss was slight.[51]

The Confederates fell back to their original position, and after a nearly four-hour fight, the engagement on the South Cavalry Field petered out. A heavy thunderstorm deluged the weary men of both sides. Merritt's command withdrew to the nearby farm of Cornelius Houghtelier, where they camped for the night.[52]

That night, Meade wired Halleck again: "My cavalry have been engaged all day on both flanks of the enemy, harassing and vigorously attacking him with great success, notwithstanding they encountered superior numbers, both of cavalry and infantry."[53] This language plainly demonstrates that Meade had not intended Kilpatrick's efforts to be decisive flanking movements, despite Kilpatrick's belief that the attacks by Farnsworth and Merritt were indeed decisive attacks. Merritt said little of this fight in his report of the Reserve Brigade's performance in the Gettysburg Campaign. He simply stated:

> I marched with the brigade about 12m. to attack the enemy's right and rear, and annoy him, while the battle was progressing on the right. I marched on the [Emmitsburg] road about four miles, where my advance

Monument to the 2nd U.S. Cavalry, directly behind Graham's guns.

"The Lost Opportunity." Looking northward toward the main Confed-
erate battle lines. It was here that the charge of the 1st and 5th U.S.
Cavalry briefly got into the Confederate rear. Note the ideal terrain for
making a mounted charge.

and skirmishers were engaged. Here the brigade drove the enemy more than a mile, routing him from strong places, stone fences, and barricades. This fight lasted about four hours (some time after the cannonading had ceased on the right), and was finally brought to a close by a heavy rain.[54]

Writing a few months after the battle, Merritt's aide-de-camp, Lt. Eugene P. Bertrand of the 6th Pennsylvania, recorded:

> The whole of the brigade bravely held the position assigned them and although they were not able to gain much advantage over the superior numbers of the enemy, yet they manfully held their ground until the evening, when they were withdrawn.[55]

The Reserve Brigade sustained 49 casualties during this fight out of 1,321 officers and men engaged, for a percentage loss of 3.1%, relatively light numbers for a four-hour battle.[56] Seventeen of those casualties came from the 2nd U. S., which lost 4.2% of its total involved, among the ten highest percentage losses of any Union cavalry regiment involved in the Battle of Gettysburg.[57] Merritt's men performed their limited assignment capably, and kept a veteran infantry brigade and three batteries of artillery busy for an entire afternoon. However, Merritt did a poor job of coordinating his attacks, and the whole action failed as a result.

The Confederate high command recognized the threat posed by this attack. Law later observed: "That General Longstreet also felt the gravest anxiety as to the result of the fighting on this flank is evidenced by the fact that he rode hastily over from the center...and, with the most marked expression of relief in his tone and manner, warmly congratulated me on the manner in which the situation had been handled."[58] Not all of the Grayclads recognized this, though. A Confederate cavalry historian gave this engagement only the most cursory of discussions:

> On the evening of the same day, the 3d, a detachment of about four hundred men, under Colonel Black, First South Carolina Cavalry, met a body of Yankee cavalry advancing from Emmettsburg [*sic*], who were attempting a demonstration against our right flank, with the support of a regiment of infantry, ambuscaded and drove them back with heavy loss.[59]

The Union high command evidently did not recognize the sterling opportunity squandered that afternoon. For a brief moment, the men of the 1st and 5th U. S. got into the Confederate rear and, with proper support, could have rolled up the Rebel line in the aftermath of the repulse of Pickett's Charge. The beaten and demoralized butternuts were as ripe for a full counterattack as any time during the entire war. A proper force of infantry, perhaps of division scale, supporting their breakthrough, could have rolled up Lee's flank and driven the Army of Northern Virginia from the field in a wild rout.

Instead, the attack was supported only by two batteries of horse artillery assigned to Farnsworth's and Merritt's Brigades. As Capt. Frederick C. Newhall of the 6th Pennsylvania pointed out:

> In fact, the operations of Merritt's brigade just at this point were not, and in the nature of things could not be of a very aggressive character. No one familiar with the circumstances can fail to see that he had far too little force to do anything but create a diversion on this flank of Lee's army which was strongly and cautiously held...A brigade of infantry backed by an army in position, will stop, if it wishes to, a brigade of cavalry outside of the lines of its own army, devoid of support, and simply moving against the enemy's flank; and neither Merritt nor the men under him had the least idea of breaking through Lee's right, alone and unsupported.[60]

Trooper Samuel Crockett of the 1st U. S. observed: "We...learned that our whole attack was a ruse and intended to make the rebels believe that the real point of attack was there while it really was on the extreme right; we were on the extreme left. If it was a ruse it succeeded for the rebels had two men there to our one and they needed them badly on the right. Our force was all cavalry, theirs in good part Infantry."[61]

Had Merritt's attack been properly coordinated with Farnsworth's, Tige Anderson's Brigade could not have been shifted to meet both threats, and the far right flank of the Confederate army would have been held by only the inadequate force of cavalry commanded by Col. Black and Hart's crippled battery. The Federal cavalry could have been used as a shock force to set the stage for an infantry assault. In a properly conceived, coordinated, executed, and supported attack, the Confederate right flank could have been rolled up and the Army driven from the field in a panic. Instead, Judson Kilpatrick cobbled together a plan, which stood little or no chance of succeeding and which unnecessarily cost Elon Farnsworth's life.

Thus ended the great Battle of Gettysburg. The final act of the climactic drama remained to be played out eight miles away, just north of the hamlet of Fairfield.

Chapter

5

"The 6th U. S. is cut to pieces..."

The Battle of Fairfield

One of Wesley Merritt's regiments of Regulars did not participate in the battle on the South Cavalry Field. The 6th U. S. Cavalry, detached from the Reserve Brigade as Cavalry Corps escort guard, was not present at Gettysburg while the struggle for the South Cavalry Field raged. Instead, it was sent on a mission to disaster.

The 6th U. S., the only Regular cavalry unit formed at the outbreak of the Civil War, was a new unit, having served for less than two years before the Battle of Gettysburg. Its men were recruited mainly from western Pennsylvania, primarily from the Pittsburgh area. Unlike their brethren in the volunteer regiments, the men of the 6th U. S. enlisted for five-year terms and were subject to the harsh discipline expected in the Regular Army. Few had prior military experience, and many were unfamiliar with the care and attention required to maintain horses. Its officers came from the various Regular cavalry regiments or from direct commissions. With inexperienced troopers and officers unaccustomed to working together, the 6th U. S. was not yet a fully cohesive command.

The commander was Maj. Samuel H. Starr, a legendary dragoon with 32 years' experience in the Regular Army by the time of the Battle of Gettysburg. Enlisting in 1832, Starr served in the engineers, infantry, and artillery before transferring to the newly-formed Second Dragoons in 1848, and worked his way up the ranks from private to officer. Commissioned a second lieutenant in 1848, he was a captain at the outbreak of the Civil War. He served briefly as colonel of a regiment of New Jersey volunteers but did not enjoy it, and so resigned his volunteer commission and went on recruiting duty in Washington after the 1862 Peninsula Campaign. He became major of the 6th U. S. on April 25, 1863, and, by virtue of his experience and rank, briefly commanded the Reserve Brigade during the early phases of the Gettysburg Campaign, until Merritt's promotion.[1] Some of his troopers believed that he was too old for the rigors of cavalry command in the field and that he was better suited to command infantry.[2] Starr, a wily old veteran, seemed to be a fine choice to command an inexperienced regiment such as the 6th U.S. Unfortunately, he was not.

Starr was known for harsh discipline toward both officers and enlisted men. One of his men noted that, "The resonances of Starr in the ways and means of inflicting degrading punishments upon the members of the command seemed to be unlimited as to number and variety." One especially unpleasant punishment involved placing an offender astride a fence, his feet tied together below, his hands tied behind his back, and his head encased in a horse's nose bag. This nasty punishment earned Starr the unflattering moniker of "Old Nose Bag."[3]

On the morning of July 3, an old farmer rode into Merritt's lines near Big Round Top and reported the presence of a large Confederate wagon train corralled in his farm field near the town of Fairfield, about eight miles behind the Confederate main line of battle. The civilian reported that the wagon train "camped all night near Fairfield without a guard of any strength"[4] and added that the moment offered "a right smart chance for you'ns to capture it, the soldiers are all over at the big fight."[5] Merritt sensed an opportunity for a kill and ordered the 6th U. S. to capture the train and hold the town of

Major Samuel H. Starr, commanding officer of the 6th U.S. Cavalry.

Monument to the 6th U.S. Cavalry on the South Cavalry Field near Graham's Battery.

Fairfield in order to cut off Lee's line of retreat. Evidently, he was comfortable with the civilian's report because he sent only one regiment—the 6th U. S.—on this mission. In fact, not all of the 6th U. S. went on this mission. One squadron, consisting of Companies D and M, was attached to Pleasonton's headquarters as its escort, leaving less than a full regiment to march behind the enemy lines.[6] Some troopers of the 6th were uncomfortable with the civilian's intelligence. One member later suggested that the old man who reported the presence of the Rebel wagon train was in fact a Confederate spy bent on setting a trap for the 6th U. S.[7]

Merritt ordered Starr to march eight to ten miles behind the Confederate lines, and "move upon the road between Fairfield and Gettysburg to keep off any supports which might be sent to Gettysburg by the enemy."[8] The Federals anticipated the fun of ransacking an unguarded Rebel supply train. Instead, a rude surprise, in the form of a brigade of Confederate cavalry, awaited Starr and his men just up the road, near the little town of Fairfield. The Regulars set out on their mission, and "[a]ll was excitement, and you will not wonder when you imagine capturing a hundred wagons laden with spoils for confiscation, and the plundering and destruction of the same."[9] The Yankees made the short ride to Fairfield in good time, with approximately 400 officers and men.[10]

It took the Regulars approximately an hour to reach their destination, with the civilian and Major Starr leading the way. One trooper recalled that, "The man seemed to be somewhat excited, emphasizing his conversation by gestures with a rawhide which he held in his right hand. Starr looked as gloomy as usual, not in the least partaking of the stranger's animation."[11] Along the way, no Rebels could be seen except a small picket post on the side of a mountain a mile or so from the road.[12] The march was pleasant. "We were supplied with luxuries which brought us thoughts of home—bread, cake, pies, etc., but the best of all were the well wishes and pleasant smiles of the fair sex, wishing us success in a glorious cause."[13] As the regiment entered the valley south of Fairfield, Starr called a halt approximately two miles from the village.

The First Squadron, made up of 60 or so troopers from two companies, was commanded by the regiment's second ranking officer, Capt. George C. Cram, a stiff-necked career Regular who was extremely unpopular with the men. Private Sidney Davis recalled: "Captain Cram was a curious capricious man seeming to be most delighted when the men most feared him.... Whenever a soldier had occasion to speak of him, his name was invariably coupled with uncomplimentary phrases. The universal desire was often thus briefly expressed, except for the religious, 'Damn Cram!'"[14] Starr ordered Cram to take the First Squadron and follow the course of an unfinished railroad, which had a north/south alignment and lay at the foot of the mountains on the western side of the narrow valley.[15] Cram's detachment reduced the effective strength of the 6th U. S. by nearly twenty percent. The rest of the regiment continued on toward the town.

As the command reached the streets of the town, the men fanned out to search for the wagon train. Lieutenant Tattnall Paulding wrote in his diary: "Arriving at Fairfield we found no train, but a few wagons which had been at the neighboring barns had left the town a few moments prior to our entering."[16] Still eager to bag the wagon train, Starr sent Lt. Christian Balder's squadron in pursuit of the wagons. Balder was a Prussian immigrant, known for his strict sense of discipline. Despite this, he was well liked by his men.[17] Balder's little column continued on, looking for the retreating wagons a mile or so out on the Fairfield-Orrtanna Road (now known as the Carroll's Tract Road). Approaching a "comfortable looking farmhouse," Balder spotted a man

*Captain George C. Cram,
6th U.S. Cavalry,
captured at Fairfield.*

in the yard of the house and called out to him, "Have you seen any rebels about here lately?"

The man did not answer right away, clearly debating the merits of responding and becoming involved. Undeterred, Balder repeated the question. This time, the man responded, "Six passed here a few minutes ago."

"What direction did they take?"

"Out that way, and up the road towards Cashtown," the man pointed north, up the Fairfield-Orrtanna Road.

As the Federals began moving off, the man stopped Balder, warning, "You had better be careful, Captain. There are many of them about here just now."

Balder responded harshly, "Is this Pennsylvania?"

"Yes, sir."

"And you farmers of Pennsylvania allow six rebels to ride unmolested about your state, and rob you just as they have a mind to?" retorted Balder. As the Federals marched off, the man gave an unintelligible reply.[18]

It is unclear to this day how many wagons were involved, since the 6th U. S. did not capture a single one. Grumble Jones wrote in his report that, "many wagons in quest of forage were already within a few hundred yards of the enemy." In the same report, he referred to "our cavalry

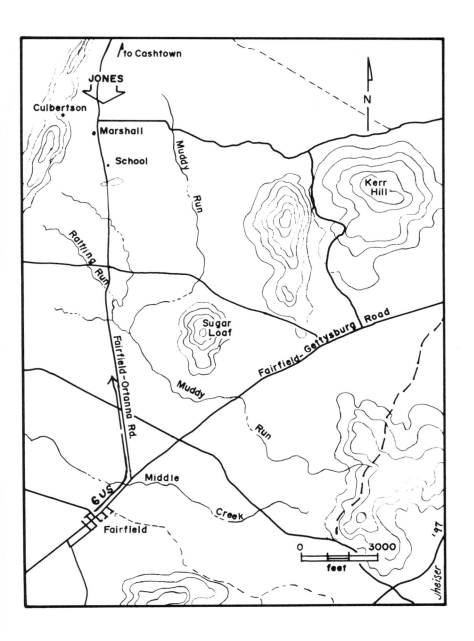

The Fairfield area.

division trains," indicating that a good number of them must have been in the area.[19] One trooper of the 6th, who was captured in the Battle of Fairfield, later claimed that he overheard a Confederate tell another prisoner that the small train was a decoy, intended to lure the Yankees into a trap.[20]

Balder's small command advanced, and eventually spotted the escaping wagons. Balder ordered his squadron to form into line of battle by companies on either side of the road, atop a small ridge, and to charge. His troopers soon encountered Jones' advance picket line of 40 or 50 dismounted men, and drove it back onto the column of wagons. The area Starr selected for his attack should have been perfect for mounted operations—a flat and narrow valley. Unfortunately the road, which should have provided a perfect lane for mounted operations, proved to be a major hindrance. The area was subdivided into farm fields and orchards lined by well-built fences, and the road was edged with high stone walls, creating a natural funnel for Balder's mounted charge.[21] Balder's men pursued the wagons for a mile or so before they suddenly halted; a large column of Jones' Brigade was approaching on the same road, with the veteran 7th Virginia Cavalry in the lead. Realizing how badly outnumbered his small command was, Balder ordered his men to turn about and return to the main body of Yankee troopers.

The Virginians spotted Balder's little column. One member of the 7th Virginia later recalled: "We had gone but a short distance when we met a squad of about thirty mounted Federal cavalrymen, who turned and ran through a lane with post and rail fence on either side."[22] Seeing an opportunity, the 7th Virginia pursued Balder's retreating men for about two miles.

With the 7th Virginia in hot pursuit, Balder located and rejoined the rest of Starr's column. After learning that a large body of gray cavalry was approaching down the Fairfield-Orrtanna Road, Starr chose to stay and fight, perhaps a sign of the more aggressive nature of the emerging commanders of the Army of the Potomac's Cavalry Corps. He ordered his outnumbered troopers to deploy into line of battle at the narrowest point in the valley. Starr ordered half of his command to dismount along a perpendicular ridgeline, taking advantage of the protection offered by a large apple orchard which sat atop the little rise. The other half stayed mounted in column along the road.[23] The position offered good fields of fire south of the Marshall farm, which sat astride the Fairfield-Orrtanna Road. There, in a 200-yard line of battle, they awaited the arrival of Grumble Jones' Brigade.

The Regulars did not have long to wait. As Starr's men finished making their dispositions, the 7th Virginia came into sight near the Marshall house, about 300 yards away. Jones spotted Starr's line of battle, took a moment to assess the position, and ordered the 7th Virginia to charge, an order its men happily obeyed. The 7th Virginia, formerly Turner Ashby's regiment, was a good unit. Private Sidney Davis later recalled that "the Seventh Virginia Cavalry [was] Ashby's pet regiment, composed of really good and well-trained soldiers, charging with drawn sabers."[24] Grumble Jones later wrote in his report: "No estimate could be made of the opposing force, but knowing a vigorous assault must put even a small force of a perfect equality with a large one until a wider field could be prepared, I at once ordered the 7th Regiment, which was in front, to charge."[25]

The men of the 7th Virginia gave a wild Rebel yell, drew their sabers with a metallic clang, and charged the Yankee position. Starr's troopers, armed with .52 caliber single-shot breechloading Sharps carbines, opened a severe fire, and blunted the 7th Virginia's attack. Hemmed in by the strong Pennsylvania fences, "too strong to be broken without an ax," the 7th Virginia suffered severely.[26] Lieutenant Col. Thomas C. Marshall, commander of the 7th Virginia, wrote in his report: "Moved up at a charge, and found the enemy strongly posted, a portion of their column in the lane, and their other forces disposed on either flank, protected on one side by an orchard and on the other by a strong post and rail fence in front. They opened a galling fire upon us, driving us back and killing and wounding a good many."[27]

Finding themselves in an ambush, the men of the 7th Virginia were forced to fight their way out of the trap created by the strong fences. They dropped out of the fight and were no factor in the remainder of the battle. The historian of Jones' Brigade, Capt. William N. McDonald, later recalled that, "Shattered and broken the head of the charging column faltered, the men behind it halted, and soon the whole regiment returned in spite of the strenuous efforts of its officers to force it forward."[28] One Yankee recalled that the fight with the 7th Virginia was not a "well-regulated fight," but rather, "a cruel, close one, where every shot from determined men told upon their opponents, who were thus jammed up between two fences and literally harmless."[29] The historian of Jones' Brigade further observed that the Yankee fire from Starr's flanks was "terrible" and that "[t]he failure of the Seventh was clearly due to the fire from the...men on the flanks, who, being unmolested, shot with deadly effect into the charging column."[30] While trying to rally the routed

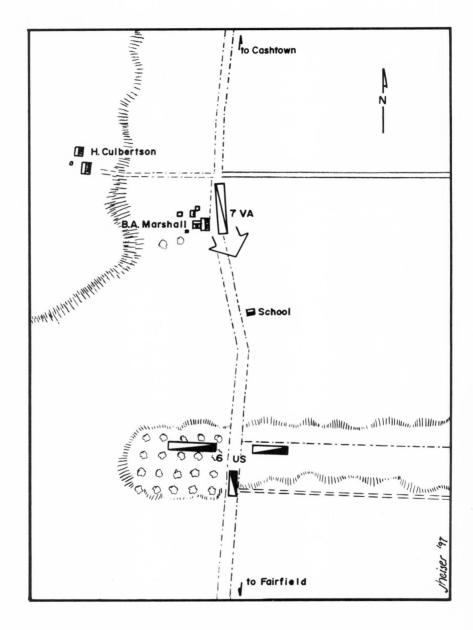

The opening of the battle in the valley north of Fairfield.

men of the 7th, Capt. John C. Shoup and his brother Lt. Jacob G. Shoup fell. Captain Shoup was seriously wounded, and Lt. Shoup was killed outright.[31]

Jones failed to reconnoiter the enemy position or to remove any of the fences which caused the 7th Virginia so much suffering. Thus, he is responsible for the disaster that befell the Seventh. Lieutenant John H. Connell of the 7th Virginia observed:

> The bravest mounted troops that ever flashed saber in sunlight now are exceedingly chary in attacking an unknown number of dismounted men, especially when they are secreted behind fences or anything that affords immunity from a cavalry charge. Every brave man who has been engaged in the mounted arm of the service will testify to the truth of this statement.[32]

Colonel Marshall wrote in his report that his "Regiment did not at this place, and time, close up as promptly as it should, in this manner, no doubt, making our losses greater than it would otherwise have been."[33] Livid over the rout of the 7th Virginia, Jones wrote that its "leading men hesitated; the regiment halted and retreated, losing more than a glorious victory would have cost had the onset been made with vigor and boldness. A failure to rally promptly and renew the fight is a blemish on the bright history of this regiment."[34] The 7th Virginia fell back 300 or 400 yards and tried to regroup.[35] As they fell back, the demoralized troopers of the regiment called out, "Boys, you are going to catch it; we have been badly beaten!"[36]

The 6th Virginia, next in Jones' column and trailed by Chew's Battery and the 11th Virginia, arrived on the field in time to watch the rout of the 7th Virginia. As they arrived, the men of the 6th Virginia heard "the carbines and revolvers of the 7th...already making music on quick time."[37] The sight of the broken ranks of the 7th Virginia unnerved some of the men of the 6th.[38] Jones ordered Chew's guns deployed in a nearby farm field; the Grayclad gunners opened fire on the Union position, several hundred yards away. Gunner George M. Neese recalled that, "We immediately put our guns in battery and opened on them, and our cavalry also opened with small arms, and for a while the conflict was fierce and hot...we had our guns in position in a wheat field where the wheat was standing thick, and nearly as high as my head, and dead ripe. It looked like a shame to have war in such a field of wheat."[39] The fire from Chew's guns was highly effective, and as Starr's men had no artillery support, the gunners went about their business unmolested. Charles F. Miller of the 6th U. S. later observed that "the shot and shell from five pieces of artillery made us think that we would better get out of there, and some of the boys made good time, too."[40]

Emboldened by the success of his initial resistance, Starr, instead of holding his strong defensive position, made a critical error and ordered Lt. Tattnall Paulding's squadron to charge, even though Paulding's men were dismounted and would have to scurry to mount up before the rest of the Regulars passed them by. Paulding recorded in his diary:

> After my men were posted behind a fence by which they were to act, I saw the enemy in great numbers forming beyond us & very soon recd an order from Maj. Starr to withdraw my men as he was about to charge and would be driven back. The men were brought in as rapidly as possible but being much tired could not go fast & before they could reach the horses our men...charged.[41]

Starr gave this order despite the fact that his men could hear the Rebel officers across the way giving orders to their men to "draw sabers."[42] The order for the Regulars to charge was Starr's second and worst mistake. "It was very unfortunate that the scattered squadrons were not withdrawn instantly from the front of such superior forces for more favorable ground. The regiment paid dearly for this error."[43] As a result of Starr's rash order, the Regulars were splintered in their unsuccessful charge.

Jones, still irate about the failure of the 7th Virginia, testily inquired, "Shall one damned regiment of Yankees whip my entire brigade?", to which the men of the 6th Virginia replied, "Let *us* try them!" Jones gave Maj. Cabell E. Fluornoy the order for an immediate charge.[44] In turn, Fluornoy told his troopers, "Men, I want every one of you to do your duty; the men that you will meet are worthy of your steel; it is the 6th Regulars, the best regiment the Yankees have."[45] E. H. Vaughn of the 6th Virginia recalled that Fluornoy's speech "rekindled some of our fire for we did not feel very good after seeing the condition the Seventh was in."[46] Roused by Jones' challenge, the men of the 6th eagerly spurred ahead. Later, Fluornoy recalled: "At the intimation of the commanding general, he gave the order to charge. The men, with a wild yell, went forward splendidly."[47]

As the charge of the 6th Virginia gained momentum, some of the routed elements of the 7th Virginia rallied and joined them. Even a detachment of the 11th Virginia joined in. With sabers flashing in the afternoon sun, the grayclad troopers swarmed toward the thin Union line. The Rebel attack caught the Federals spread out with their flanks uncovered by the rash charge ordered and personally led by Starr. Starr's unwise charge quickly turned into a retreat as the badly outnumbered Federals scampered back toward their main line of battle. Nevertheless, the beleaguered Federals continued their resistance, occasionally inflicting serious damage on the pursuing Confederates. Sergeant T. J. Young of the 6th Virginia was badly wounded. "Just as we entered the wheat field where the dismounted Federals were a bullet struck me a little below the right corner of my mouth and penetrated deep enough to knock out two of my teeth and break my jawbone."[48] Somehow, Sgt. Young survived this horrendous wound.

As the charge of the 6th Virginia neared the Yankee's line in the apple orchard, Lt. John Blue noted: "As we neared the orchard we became convinced that something more than apples were to be found in that orchard." The advancing Rebels got orders not to fire until they were face to face with the enemy.[49] The adjutant of the 6th Virginia, Lt. John Allan, was shot from the saddle during the charge of his regiment, dying in the midst of the whirling fight. Private John N. Opie of the 6th Virginia later recalled that Allan, apparently anticipating that the next fight would be his last, wrote a note the night before, asking that his body be delivered to his father in Baltimore and promising that anyone who did would be paid a reward of $500. Opie recalled: "We delivered his body, together with the note, to a citizen and afterwards learned that he carried out the request and received the money. This is one of the many instances I know of where men had a premonition of death."[50]

As the Confederates struck Starr's thin line, the Yankee troopers fired rapidly from the orchard, "wasting ammunition, and emptying their arms, most of their shots passed over our heads."[51] The fight quickly turned into a hand-to-hand melee with sabers and pistols used at short range. Opie described how,

Col. Lunsford Lomax, commander of the 11th Virginia Cavalry, (shown as Brig. Gen.).

"The boys rode, sabre in hand, right into the Sixth Regulars, sabering right and left as they went.... A great many of the enemy were knocked from their horses with the sabre but succeeded in escaping through the tall wheat, which had not yet been harvested."[52]

Blue noted that the Regulars were "stubborn fighters, rather inclined to be mulish and hard to drive."[53] One veteran of the 6th U. S. remembered:

> ...the Sixth Virginia Cavalry charged down on the Sixth U. S. Cavalry, and they being dismounted, and having deployed in fighting the Seventh Virginia Cavalry, were taken at great disadvantage, as most of them were unable to reach and remount their horses, and, as a result, it became a desperate hand to hand struggle....[54]

Federal trooper Charles F. Miller recalled:

> The old saying is, "Those who know nothing fear nothing," and I confess the fact that two comrades and myself, through sheer, reckless excitement, not bravery, not even thinking our lives were in danger, confronted twice our number at no more than 15 yards distance, and exchanged salutations with them with Colts navy revolvers. We were not an easy prey as they had anticipated, as two of their number fell on the spot, and the other four putting spurs to their steeds fled. Looking around, we found ourselves alone; the whole command had vanished and we were being flanked, so we dashed on after the retreating column, passing through an orchard into a lane. We saw a greycoat advancing near a barn, and by his careless manner it was evident that he had not seen us. By agreement we halted and leveled our carbines to surprise the chap as he rounded the corner, and I think he was surprised by the report of the three guns the contents of which brought both horse and man to the ground. We did not stop to see whether he was hurt or not but put spurs to our horses hoping to gain the road and overtake the column.[55]

Another Federal, Private Joseph Charlton, was wounded while mounted during the early phase of the fight. A Rebel bullet lodged in his right hip. Rapidly losing strength and afraid of falling from his horse, Charlton tried to dismount along a fence line. Succeeding in dismounting but weakened by the loss of blood, he slipped and fell on the fence, breaking three ribs. In intense pain, weak from his wounds, Charlton was unable to stand. "With head swinging down on one side and feet on the other, and blood streaming from his wound, poor Joe hung" on the fence until a comrade came along, freed Charlton from his trap, and carried him down the road to a nearby farmhouse, where he was left behind.[56]

Lieutenant Balder's isolated squadron was consumed by the Confederate charge, and Balder, after refusing a demand for surrender, pulled his saber and charged toward the Rebels, who allowed him to pass through their lines and swarmed around him, firing their pistols. Balder, mortally wounded by a pistol ball, managed to escape and rode into the town. There, two citizens helped him from his horse and onto their porch, where he sat in a chair, his face pale, his eyes closed, and suffering intense pain. After the battle, a Federal trooper found him there, and asked if he was hurt. Mustering all of his strength and self-discipline, Balder replied, "Corporal, tell the men to save themselves." He died after several days of agony.[57]

Major Starr, riding with Balder, tried to cut his way out of the fight with his saber but was felled by the combination of a saber lick to the head and a severe bullet wound to his arm. The arm eventually required amputation. Lieutenant R. R. Duncan of Company B of the 6th Virginia, whose saber stroke unhorsed Starr, proceeded to saber two more Yankees, running his sword all the way through one and "twisting him from his horse."[58]

The rest of the Regulars suffered greatly in this attack. Lieutenant John B. Connell of the 7th Virginia recorded:

> Many [of the Regulars] jumped off their horses and concealed themselves in the tall grass; but this strategy was soon detected as we had a great many more horses than prisoners, so we commenced a search, and I shall never forget how ludicrous the soldiers looked as they popped up out of the grass as we approached them. Neither shall I forget one beardless youth that particularly attracted my attention and deepest sympathy. He was badly wounded, and was also suffering from the effects of heat and thirst. We gave him water and placed him in as comfortable a position as possible. He had an honest face, a brave heart....[59]

Lieutenant Tattnall Paulding of the 6th U. S. ordered his squadron, which had been fighting dismounted, to mount. His men were in the process of doing so when the Confederate charge crashed into their ranks. Mounted Rebels ran down the dismounted Yankees, using their sabers "mercilessly," scattering Paulding's command "through the field on the right of the road or on the left as we were now going, and being pursued by the mounted foe were soon captured."[60]

Private Charles F. Miller was one of the Federals captured. After having his horse shot out from under him, Miller was thrown to the ground. He crawled to a nearby fence, and, with only one cartridge for his carbine, "leveled my piece on a rail, and taking slow and deliberate aim I fired. This delay was disastrous on my part, for if I had taken to my heels as soon as my horse fell, possibly I might have escaped, but now they were too close upon me. I did, however, run until my breath was exhausted, unmindful of the shots which struck around me, and the commands to halt, surrender, etc." Miller reached his company, but the sheer weight of the Confederate numbers soon left the entire company little choice but to surrender. Miller trudged off behind the Rebel lines, now a prisoner of war.[61]

Another Federal, Private Sidney Davis, had a similar story. Davis, who had a new carbine, tried to hide the weapon in the tall grass and drew his revolver. Leaning against a fence and feigning being badly wounded, Davis awaited the Confederate approach. One butternut trooper called to him, "Take off those belts!" Instead, Davis raised his revolver and tried to fire at the approaching enemy. His cartridges spoiled by dampness, the cap failed to fire, and the gun did not discharge. Davis realized that the game was up. When the leader of the Confederates said, "Come across the fence, and give up your arms," Davis complied.[62]

However, as Davis was marched off to begin his tenure as a prisoner of war, he looked back and spotted a wounded Confederate trooper, whose plight caught his eye. Davis recalled:

> He was lying on his stomach, partially raised up on his elbows, while from his breast a steady stream of blood was flowing. His ghastly face was turned towards me, and his eyes regarded me with glaring intensity, so full of defiant, disdainful expression. Could it be that my bullet had stricken him down, and that, by some mysterious intuition, he had tracked me out?

Davis trudged off, the image burned forever in his brain.[63] The same fate befell the Yankee troopers holding the orchard. Although their rapid firing carbines held off the Rebels for a short time, they were vastly outnumbered and easily flanked. Lieutenant Blue recalled:

> We finally persuaded them to follow the rest of their line, which had already been driven back some distance by the 7th regiment on our right. When they left the orchard their line was badly broken and we gave them no time to reform and soon had them on the run on the road leading in the direction of Fairfield. Their running qualities were fully equal to their fighting.[64]

The Yankee troopers in the orchard evidently never received orders to mount or to try to escape. They were overwhelmed by the mounted charge.

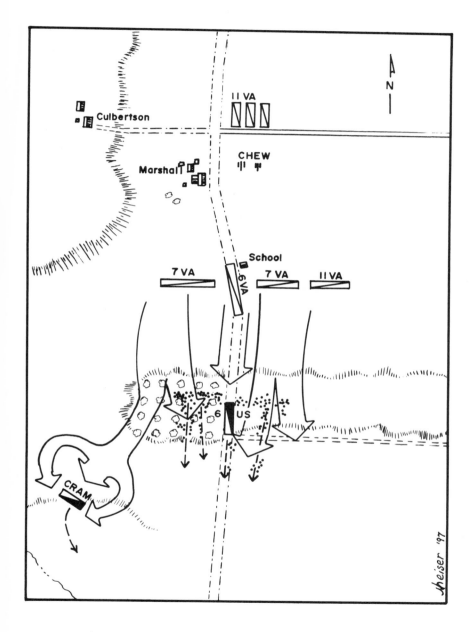

The 6th U.S. Cavalry being overwhelmed by Jones' Brigade.

One of the wounded Yankee officers captured in the orchard was a young Ohioan, Lt. Adna R. Chaffee. Lieutenant Chaffee was a career Regular who commanded a company of the 6th U.S. The Confederates tried to parole Chaffee, but he refused a parole in the field, obeying a recent War Department directive that the men of the 6th U.S. not give

Lt. Adna R. Chaffee,
6th U.S. Cavalry, wounded and
captured at Fairfield.

their paroles if captured. The frustrated Confederates, concerned that they could not manage their large haul of prisoners, simply left Chaffee behind with the other wounded. Chaffee was found lying on the ground in the orchard, being tended to by one of his men, a "neatly cut crimson edged hole in his blue pantaloons over the front part of his thigh. He was quite cheerful."[65] As a reward for his gallantry in the fighting and for his steadfast refusal to give his parole, Chaffee was brevetted to first lieutenant, effective July 3, 1863.[66]

Chaffee went on to have a long and distinguished career in the Regular Army, eventually achieving the rank of major general of volunteers in the Spanish-American War.[67] He commanded the U.S. contingent in the Peking relief expedition during the Boxer Rebellion, and toward the end of his career, he served as chief of staff of the U. S. Army, the army's top position in those days. His son, Maj. Gen. Adna R. Chaffee, Jr., also a career cavalryman, was the first commander of the United States Army's Armored Corps during World War II and gave Gen. George S. Patton, Jr., his first armored command.

Lieutenant Louis H. Carpenter of the 6th U. S. recalled: "At the fight near Fairfield, I thought several times that I was destined to be an inmate of Libby Prison. But I made up my mind that I would be badly wounded first at any rate. At one time I was entirely surrounded in the town itself, but I managed to cut my way out." In the process, Carpenter lost his saber and his bridle in the fight, but was fortunate enough to capture a replacement bridle during the melee at Fairfield. The saber was not replaced until July 7th, when he captured a replacement from another trooper of Jones' Brigade.[68]

The Yankee resistance quickly collapsed, and the overwhelmed blue troopers were captured in masses. One Yankee, Ran R. Knapp, wrote in his diary that night, "Regt went to Fairfield wher we attacked & was Repulsed had a very hot fight fought a Brgade of Cv & drove them to the Infantry and Arty support where we...out as flankers to the left of the road were flanked & surrounded and had to Cut our way out run the gauntlet in fine style & most of us succeede in gett-out."[69] The Yankees put up a stubborn fight in the orchard, but the strength of the Confederate assault soon set those lucky enough to escape the saber running toward the town of Fairfield.

Recognizing the danger to his comrades, a Yankee squadron commander ordered his mounted men to charge from the road into the melee swirling in the orchard. Instead of relieving the pressure, this move only provided the Rebels with more available prisoners. The 6th U. S. might have lost its regimental colors in this charge, but for the quick action of Sgt. George C. Platt, who grabbed the flag from the color bearer and "sticking close to the fence, put spurs to his horse," rescuing the colors from certain capture.[70] Platt was awarded the Medal of Honor,

Modern view of the Fairfield battlefield.

for seizing "the regimental flag upon the death of the standard bearer in a hand-to-hand fight and prevented it from falling into the hands of the enemy."[71]

By now, the Regulars were completely routed, their remaining elements fleeing for the town of Fairfield, many with Confederates in hot pursuit. Lieutenant Paulding tried to escape on his horse but encountered difficulties created by the terrain:

> Finding it impossible to get away with my horse I left him between a ditch and a fence both impassable and climbing the fence took it on foot through the field pursued by half a dozen the enemy's mounted men. They were soon on each side of me & being much blown by hard running & seeing no possibility of escape I surrendered to a man who was vociferously demanding my surrender & who at once robbed me of my field glass.[72]

Paulding was taken to the rear, where his journey to Richmond's infamous Libby Prison began. When he arrived at the Marshall house, Paulding found a number of the regiment's officers lying wounded, including Starr.[73]

Meanwhile the lost squadron of Capt. George C. Cram approached the field after their detour along the railroad bed. Hearing the nearby battle rage, the Yankees rode to the sound of the guns, where they spotted Starr's routed troopers fleeing toward Fairfield. In an attempt to relieve the pressure on his compatriots, Cram ordered his men to charge into the fray. The attack was futile, and Cram's command was quickly absorbed by the Confederates. Cram was captured, leaving Lt. Nicholas Nolan as the senior Yankee officer on the field.

Nolan recalled in his report: "I being the only officer then left with the squadron, took command. I found I was entirely cut off from the regiment, and had the enemy on both flanks and rear of me."[74] Nolan, desperate for information on the rest of the regiment, sent Sgt. Martin Schwenk to cut his way through to the rest of the Yankee command. Schwenk somehow made it through the lines but was unable to locate any other officer.[75] He was awarded the Medal of Honor for his "bravery in an attempt to carry a communication through the enemy's lines" and for rescuing "an officer from the hands of the enemy."[76] Some of Nolan's men tried to free their captured officers, and Pvt. Patrick Kelly made an unsuccessful effort to capture the colors of the 6th Virginia. Overwhelmed by superior Rebel numbers, Nolan ordered his men to withdraw. "After the regiment was repulsed from [Fairfield], I immediately commenced 'retreating,' disputing every inch of ground with the enemy. Finding the enemy in force, I gradually fell back in the direction of Mechanicstown, where I found the regiment, and also ascertained that the commanding officer was wounded and in the hands of the enemy."[77]

The Confederates pursued the fleeing Yankees for about three miles, through the streets of the town, to the entrance of Fairfield Gap, where they finally gave up the chase. Lieutenant Blue observed: "The chase was soon given up, General Jones no doubt feared being led into a trap." In fact, Lt. Louis H. Carpenter of the 6th U. S. managed to rally some of the routed Federals three times in half a mile, checking Jones' advance and driving him back through the town. By this time, Carpenter had only 100 men with him, and Nolan an additional fifty.[78] Their ardor for the chase thus chilled, Jones' Brigade then went into camp.[79] The remnants of the 6th U. S. fled all the way to Emmitsburg, where its survivors found elements of the rest of the Reserve Brigade.

Along the way, the two forces collided periodically. The 6th Virginia Cavalry ran into Federal troopers near the town of Greencastle, Pennsylvania that night. Courier W. T. Kerfoot, of the 6th Virginia Cavalry, who had no saber as a result of a broken arm, and who had emptied his pistol during the melee at Fairfield, was with his unit when the Yankees attacked. Another whirling skirmish ensued in the darkness, with "the men so mixed up that it was hard to tell friend from foe." Kerfoot received a saber slash to the forehead and tried to ward off another with his hand. Instead, the Northern saber cut off one of his fingers, and Kerfoot, in pain and bleeding profusely, rode off with cries of "Surrender!" echoing in his ears. Escaping, Kerfoot found another wounded Rebel in a grove of dense undergrowth, and the two Southerners eventually escaped. Years later, Kerfoot recognized how lucky he was to have survived with only the loss of a finger.[80]

The fight at Fairfield had been severe. The 6th U. S., numbering about 400 men and officers at the beginning of the battle, suffered nearly 60% casualties, including six killed, 28 wounded, and 208 captured. Only two officers, Lts. Nolan and Carpenter, escaped. Major Starr lost an arm, while Balder died of his wounds several days later.[81] Despite this, the Regulars had fought hard. Sergeant Michael C. Gorman killed five Confederates and captured another two single-handedly.[82] A bronze plaque adorns the small home in Fairfield where Balder spent his last days, and a street in the town is named for him. Despite the debacle at

Fairfield, Starr was brevetted to colonel for his performance during the Gettysburg Campaign. He did not return to duty until November, when he was exchanged by the Confederates.[83] One member of the 1st U. S. wrote in his diary on July 3: "The 6th U. S. is cut to pieces; there are less than a hundred of them left."[84] He was right—when the bugles sounded reveille on the morning of July 4, only one officer and 84 enlisted men answered its call.[85]

Less than a week later, the 6th U. S. and Jones' Brigade tangled again at Funkstown, Maryland. At Funkstown, the 7th Virginia avenged itself for its poor performance at Fairfield. Jones crowed, "the Seventh Virginia... availed itself of the opportunity of settling old scores. Sabers were used freely...and the road of slumbering wrath was marked here and there by cleft skulls and pierced bodies. The day at Fairfield is fully and nobly avenged. The Sixth Regular Cavalry numbers among the things that were."[86] This statement was false—the Sixth fought in most of the major cavalry engagements for the remainder of the war. Nevertheless, it suffered greatly at the hands of Jones' Brigade during the Gettysburg Campaign, and its percentage of losses rank among the highest of either army. The debacle at Fairfield was the only blemish on the superb performance of the Federal cavalry in the Gettysburg Campaign.

Jones' losses were far less. Of 1,600 men in his brigade, Jones reported casualties totaling 58 killed, wounded, and missing. The 6th Virginia lost 28 men, the 7th Virginia lost 30, and neither the 11th Virginia nor Chew's Battery reported any casualties. This fight was almost completely one-sided.[87] Jones' men performed well that day, as they did throughout the entire Gettysburg Campaign. It may be argued that Jones' men gave the best performance of all the Confederate cavalry during the invasion of Pennsylvania. In fact, the Battle of Fairfield was one of the few highlights for the Confederate mounted arm, which received a number of bloody noses over the course of the campaign.

Embarrassed by the debacle at Fairfield, Merritt tried to soften the magnitude of his defeat when he wrote his report of Gettysburg. He wrote:

> In the meantime, Major Starr and the Sixth U. S. Cavalry, was detached with his regiment toward Fairfield or Millerstown; engaged a superior force of the enemy, not without success. His regiment lost heavily in officers and men, and I regret to say that the Major himself—than whom there is no more gallant officer in the service—was seriously wounded, losing an arm.[88]

In a March 1864 letter, Merritt's aide, Lt. Eugene P. Bertrand, wrote, "The 6th U. S. Cavalry met a vastly superior force of the enemy near Fairfield, and although they severely punished the enemy, they were finally obliged to withdraw."[89]

George W. Cooper, of Company E of the 6th U. S., writing many years later, summed it up well: "The meeting of the two forces was a surprise to both. General Jones was coming down from his Chambersburg raid. The 6th went up that morning from Emmittsburg [sic] to try to capture a foraging train of the enemy and met Jones' Brigade and got badly whipped."[90] Trooper James Lowden of Company M, 6th U. S., believed that his regiment actually tangled with a larger force; 28 years after the battle, he wrote that the Regulars had taken on two brigades of cavalry and two batteries of artillery, and that the men of the 6th U. S., "for several hours successfully withstood and repulsed charge after charge, although nine-tenths of them were killed, wounded, or taken prisoners."[91]

In a letter to E. H. Vaughn of the 6th Virginia, Sidney Davis wrote: "We who were beaten don't get much satisfaction out of this phase of the affair, yet we know now that it wasn't all our fault."[92] Vaughn later replied, "We defeated you, it is true, but harder fighting we never did, nor heavier losses ever suffer than on this field; in short, it was a victory by defeat."[93] That two Regulars were awarded the Medal of Honor that afternoon is a good indication of the ferocity of this brief fight.

The Regulars were not bitter about their defeat at the hands of Grumble Jones. Twenty-five years later, one old Regular recalled:

> Ask a member of the Sixth U. S. Cavalry a question about Fairfield, and you will see his eyes gleam; he knows he gave his regiment and Fairfield a place in the history of his country, of which neither he nor the citizens of Fairfield need be ashamed—that is the secret of his love for this beautiful valley.[94]

Merritt deserves much of the blame for the debacle at Fairfield. Ordering a lone regiment to go on a raid far behind enemy lines without recent intelligence is contrary to good practice. If Merritt was inclined to order such a raid, he should have sent an appropriately large force to accomplish the goal. A single regiment was bound to fail, and fail it did. At the same time, the decision to send Starr's lone regiment to Fairfield was consistent with the new, aggressive philosophy of hard marching and hard fighting encouraged by the high command of the Army of the Potomac's Cavalry Corps during the Gettysburg Campaign. The 6th U.S.

fought hard at Fairfield and resisted stoutly, as did the balance of the Army of the Potomac, just a few miles away at Gettysburg.

With the repulse of Starr's Regulars, the last chapter of the Battle of Gettysburg came to a close. With the close of the battle came the recriminations. Upon reflection, it is clear that a great opportunity was squandered at Fairfield by the command of the Federal cavalry on July 3.

Modern views of Fairfield. The house (above) where Major Starr was taken after the battle and a church (below) that was used as a hospital.

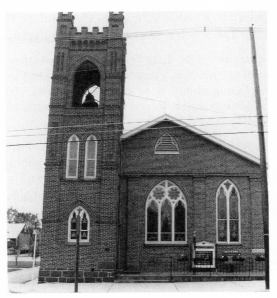

Jones's Brigade marker located north of Fairfield on Carroll's Tract Road.

In 1909 the survivors of the 6th U.S. Cavalry erected this plaque in front of the Marshall House.

Conclusion

"It was a useless waste of life, and the charge never should have been made...."

The Confederate high command realized that it had dodged a bullet on South Cavalry Field. Writing many years after the war, James Longstreet observed:

> Kilpatrick's mistake was not putting Farnsworth in on Merritt's left, where he would have had an open ride, and made more trouble than was ever made by a cavalry brigade. Had the ride been followed by prompt advance of the enemy's infantry in line beyond our right and pushed with vigor, they could have reached our line of retreat. General Meade ordered his left, but delay in getting the orders and preparing to get through the rough grounds consumed time, and the move was abandoned. The Fifth and Sixth Corps were in convenient position, and would have had good ground for marching after getting out of the rocky fastnesses of Round Top.[1]

Lt. Gen. James Longstreet.

Law echoed this, noting that, "General Longstreet, aware of the danger that threatened our right from the attack of Kilpatrick's division, came over to my position late in the afternoon, and expressed his satisfaction at the result and the promptness and good conduct of the troops engaged."[2] In 1914, Law commented:

> Pickett's fatal attack had just been repulsed; my flanking line, which covered the right-rear of our army, had been stretched to its utmost limit, being reduced to a mere skirmish line in many places. If under these circumstances, General Kilpatrick had thrown Farnsworth's entire brigade through the gap in my line where the First Vermont Cavalry had entered,

and at the same time had attacked with the full strength of Merritt's Brigade up the Emmitsburg Road, on which it was in position, the result must have been disastrous to that wing of our army at least.[3]

And Henry Benning commented:

> Brigadier-General E. M. Law, who commanded the division, General Hood having been wounded the day before, made the disposition to receive this cavalry. At very short notice he put the artillery across the road, the Seventh Georgia beside the road in a wood a little distance beyond the artillery, and the Ninth Georgia in a wood at some distance on the other side of the road and of the enclosed field. These two regiments were very small, having suffered heavily the day before. They were all that could be spared from the line of battle, and to spare them was a risk. Lee's baggage and rear were saved. There was nothing else to protect them. This was an exploit which excited my admiration. Never was anything better managed.[4]

At the climax of Pickett's Charge, looking to support the temporary breach in the Federal line along Cemetery Ridge, Robert E. Lee reportedly asked, "Where is Law's Division? Where is Hood with his spirited Texans?"[5] They were pinned down, defending against the cavalry attacks, effectively removed from the main fray. Lieutenant Col. John W. Phillips of the 18th Pennsylvania Cavalry commented:

> Then, when the fierce contest was raging...the threat on the right became a danger, and instead of sending aid toward the center, where the fate of the battle was being decided in a death grapple, or attacking the line on his front as a diversion in favor of the attacking column in the center, he was compelled to turn and make defense on his right side.[6]

Kilpatrick was also aware of the lost opportunity. When he penned his report of the battle, he wrote:

> Previous to the attack, the enemy had made a most fierce and determined attack on the left of our main line of battle, with the view to turn it. We hope we assisted in preventing this. I am of the opinion that, had our infantry on my right advanced at once when relieved from the enemy's attack in their front, the enemy could not have recovered from the confusion into which Generals Farnsworth and Merritt had thrown them, but would have rushed back, one division upon another, until, instead of a defeat, a total rout would have ensued.[7]

Because he was the architect of these attacks, it is interesting to see what the benefit of perfect hindsight did for Kilpatrick. It is a shame he did not recognize the opportunity when it presented itself. Instead of using Farnsworth's Brigade to pin down the Confederate infantry by sending it forward dismounted, Kilpatrick ordered a mounted charge over some of the most wretched ground imaginable. Rather than taking advantage of the flat, open fields in front of Merritt and ordering a concentrated mounted charge around the nearly undefended Confederate flank, Kilpatrick wasted the lives of brave men by launching uncoordinated and unsupported assaults that were destined to fail. Further, the Federal Sixth Corps was just north of the area chosen by Kilpatrick for his attack and was mostly fresh. Two of its divisions had not seen action during the battle. In his report of the Gettysburg Campaign, Maj. Gen. John Sedgwick, commander of the Sixth Corps, stated, "During [Pickett's Charge], the troops were more or less exposed to the fire of the enemy's artillery, but, with the exception of the evening of July 2, they were at no time seriously engaged."[8] Had Meade ordered the Sixth Corps forward to support Kilpatrick's attacks, the tide of the battle would have changed. In addition, the Federal Second and Fifth Corps, although battered on July 2 and July 3, were still full of fight and ready to advance in a determined counterattack. The preoccupied Confederates, battered from the repulse of Pickett's Charge, might not have been able to fend off a determined attack.

Major Gen. Abner Doubleday, the senior division commander in the First Corps of the Army of the Potomac, wrote:

> When Pickett's Charge was repulsed, and the whole plain covered with fugitives, we all expected that Wellington's command at Waterloo of "Up, guards, up and at them!" would be repeated, and that a grand counter-charge would be made. But General Meade had made no arrangements to give a return thrust. It seems to me that he should have posted the Sixth and part of the Twelfth Corps in rear of [Brig. Gen. John] Gibbon's division the moment Pickett's infantry was seen emerging from the woods, a mile and a half off. If they broke through our centre these corps would have been there to receive them, and if they failed to pierce our line and retreated, the two corps could have followed them up promptly before they had time to rally and reorganize.... In all probability we would have cut the enemy's army in two, and captured the long line of batteries opposite us, which were but slightly guarded...Meade...recognized in some sort the good effects of a counter-blow; but to be effective the movement should have been prepared beforehand.... A counter-charge under such circumstances is considered almost imperative in war, for the beaten army, running and dismayed, cannot, in the nature of things, resist with much spirit; whereas, the pursuers, highly elated by their success, and with the prospect of ending the contest, fight with more energy and bravery.[9]

The attacks by Farnsworth and Merritt had the makings of the counterattack described by Doubleday. Had they been properly supported by infantry, Lee's army could have been split in two and defeated.

Alternatively, the charge did manage to pierce the Confederate lines for a short time. Had Merritt's attack been properly coordinated with Farnsworth's, Tige Anderson's Brigade could not have been shifted to meet threats, and the far right flank of the Rebel army would have been held by only Col. Black's small force of cavalry and Hart's crippled battery. In a properly conceived, executed, and supported attack, the Confederate right flank could have been rolled up and the Army of Northern Virginia driven from the field. Instead, Kilpatrick failed to detect this weakness and cobbled together a fatally flawed plan which stood little chance of succeeding.

Even Federal troopers who did not participate in Farnsworth's Charge recognized its futility. Private Silas D. Wesson of the 8th Illinois Cavalry of Buford's Division, who served in Farnsworth's old company, noted in his diary on July 5: "Kilpatrick...ordered him to make an attack. He knew he could not win."[10] More importantly, Farnsworth's troopers also recognized the futility of their sacrifice. W. J. Brown of Company B, 1st West Virginia Cavalry, stated that, "I think it was a useless waste of life, and the charge should never have been made. No one knew this any better than Farnsworth."[11] One Illinois historian observed about Farnsworth: "His young life was full of high promise—suddenly going out."[12] Farnsworth's old friend James H. Kidd observed:

> Had he lived, the brave young Illiniosan might have been another Custer. He had all the qualities needed to make a great career—youth, health, a noble physique, courage, patriotism, ability and rank. He was poised, like Custer, and had discretion as well as dash. They were a noble pair, and nobly did they justify the confidence reposed in them. One lived to court death on scores of battle fields, winning imperishable laurels in them all; the other was cut down in the very beginning of his brilliant carrer, but his name will forever be associated with what is destined to be in the history of the most memorable battle of the war, and the one from which is dated the beginning of the downfall of the Confederate cause, and the complete restoration of the Union.[13]

Farnsworth himself was a great loss to the Union, a victim of Kilpatrick's ambitions.

Likewise, Merritt's attack could have accomplished much more. For a short time, the men of the 1st and 5th U. S. flanked Lee's line and had an opportunity to roll up the Southern line in the aftermath of Pickett's

Charge. The demoralized Confederates were as ripe for a full counter-attack as at any time during the entire war. Alfred Pleasonton recognized the need for infantry support. When he testified before the Congressional Committee on the Conduct of the War, he commented, "I urged [General Meade] to order a general advance of the whole army in pursuit of the enemy, for I was satisfied that the Rebel army was not only demoralized, but that they must be nearly, if not quite, out of ammunition; and that our army, being in fine spirits with this last repulse, could have easily defeated and routed the enemy."[14]

Instead, Merritt's attack was supported only by the two batteries of horse artillery attached to his brigade and Farnsworth's. As Capt. Frederick C. Newhall of the 6th Pennsylvania astutely pointed out, "A brigade of infantry backed by an army in position, will stop, if it wishes to, a brigade of cavalry outside of the lines of its own army, devoid of support, and simply moving against the enemy's flank; and neither Merritt nor the men under him had the least idea of breaking through Lee's right, alone and unsupported."[15] Trooper Samuel Crockett of the 1st U. S. observed:

> We...learned that our whole attack was a ruse and intended to make the rebels believe that the real point of attack was there while it was on the extreme right; we were on the extreme left. If it was a ruse it succeeded for the rebels had 10 men there for our one and they needed them badly on the right. Our force was all cavalry, theirs in good part Infantry.[16]

Brevet Brig. Gen. Theophilus F. Rodenbough, who as a young captain commanded the 2nd U. S. in the fight for South Cavalry Field, became the leading American cavalry authority later in life. In an 1889 article entitled "Cavalry War Lessons," Rodenbough commented:

> The Confederate testimony shows clearly (a) that the two small cavalry brigades of Merritt and Farnsworth so fully engaged the attention of Law's infantry division that its support of Pickett (at one time contemplated by Longstreet) was out of the question, although such timely support would have rendered the famous assault of more avail even if it had not seriously affected the general issue; (b) that an active cooperation of the Union infantry near Kilpatrick upon Law's attenuated front would have a good chance of turning the Confederate flank and of "doubling up" Longstreet's already disintegrated corps. It is fair to assume that mounted operations alone would not have been so successful, as the combination of vigorous fighting on foot by Merritt and the threatening mounted demonstrations by Farnsworth—although the latter were carried to excess.[17]

Edwin B. Coddington, the preeminent historian of the Gettysburg Campaign, commented:

> [Farnsworth] put on a brilliant display of courage and horsemanship, but the attack ended in a fiasco, including the death of Farnsworth. If Kilpatrick had assumed that Law's men were demoralized by the repulse of Pickett and Pettigrew, he was sadly mistaken.... The fault in this instance lay in part with Meade for not putting Sedgwick in overall command of the forces on the extreme left and giving him instructions to take advantage of any weakness in enemy resistance without awaiting orders from headquarters. But neither can Pleasonton escape responsibility, for he should have alerted Federal commanders to Kilpatrick's operations and asked them to cooperate. Nevertheless, Kilpatrick's complaint about the inactivity of Union infantry does not excuse him from the charge of bad generalship.[18]

Finally, the Confederate cavalry was pinned down by Gregg and Custer a few miles away at the East Cavalry Field, so there were no Confederate cavalry forces available to oppose a determined counterattack. While it is easy to enjoy the benefit of hindsight, it is clear that an opportunity to destroy Lee's army was briefly in the hands of the Army of the Potomac on the afternoon of July 3. The opportunity was allowed to slip away by bad command decisions by Kilpatrick and Meade. Although Gettysburg was clearly a Union victory, it could have been more.

Likewise, a prime opportunity was squandered at Fairfield. Had Merritt detached a significant force, such as the entire Reserve Brigade, it could have taken and held Fairfield Gap and Monterey Pass, constricting Lee's line of retreat toward Maryland. This move would have given the Army of the Potomac an opportunity to destroy the beaten Army of Northern Virginia. In order to escape to Virginia via the most direct route, Lee would have been required to fight his way through strongly defended Union positions on the high ground above Monterey Pass, or make a significant detour to Cashtown Gap, several miles to the north and west. A delaying action by dismounted cavalrymen might have bought sufficient time for the Army of the Potomac's infantry to come up, and the decisive battle of the Civil War could have occurred at the mouth of Monterey Pass. Colonel William C. Oates of the 15th Alabama observed:

> Had Meade drawn on his heavy reserves immediately after Lee's repulse on the third day and sent 40,000 men to intercept his communications, block the mountain passes and thus obstruct his line of retreat toward the Potomac and Virginia, and when he began to move have pressed hard

on his rear, he would have crippled Lee much worse than he did and with some probability of his destruction. But that general was so delighted that he did not get whipped at Gettysburg and so carried away with the renown of having repulsed and turned Lee homeward that he thought it wise to let well enough alone and thus he lost a great opportunity.[19]

The Union high command missed the opportunity presented at Fairfield entirely. Instead, Merritt sent an unsupported regiment on a raid for booty far behind enemy lines, and his men paid the price for his mistake. Further, Major Starr mismanaged the battle and made a bad situation far worse. Instead of withdrawing when faced with the overwhelming numerical superiority of Grumble Jones' Brigade, Starr chose to stay and fight. The Yankee debacle at Fairfield became inevitable at the moment Starr made his decision.

Despite the failures on July 3, Wesley Merritt and Judson Kilpatrick both escaped censure. In Merritt's case, his status as a particular favorite of both Pleasonton and Buford doubtless insulated him from criticism. Despite his poor performance on July 3, Merritt achieved division command in December 1863, upon John Buford's death. He served as the surrender officer at Appomattox and later commanded the 5th and 9th U. S. Cavalry Regiments after the Civil War. Followed by a stint as commandant of the U. S. Military Academy at West Point, Merritt's long and extremely distinguished career in the Regular Army climaxed with the capture of Manila in 1898. Despite these accomplishments, Wesley Merritt had a poor day on July 3. He made unwise decisions in both phases—in the timing of his attacks on South Cavalry Field and in sending the 6th U. S. to disaster at Fairfield. Perhaps the magnitude of the Federal victory at Gettysburg insulated him, or perhaps his newness to command allowed him some additional margin for error which he otherwise might not have had.

Similarly, Judson Kilpatrick was not criticized. Kilpatrick made poor choices in ordering Elon Farnsworth's attack and in choosing the terrain for his attacks. Despite having lived up to his unflattering nickname of "Kill-cavalry," he has escaped with little criticism. This is somewhat baffling, as he appears to have had only a handful of successful days in the entire course of the war. Certainly July 3, 1863, cannot number among those few good days. Rather, this was Judson Kilpatrick at his very worst. Impulsive and always searching for opportunities for self-aggrandizement, his ambition cost the life of a brave and promising young general, as well as the men who followed him into battle, for no good reason.

Shortly after the end of the Battle of Gettysburg, riots broke out in New York City over conscription. Perhaps as punishment for causing Farnsworth's death, Kilpatrick was sent to New York to assume command of the Federal cavalry forces gathered there to restore order. In the spring of 1864, he, along with Col. Ulric Dahlgren, led a failed raid on Richmond which was intended to free Union prisoners from Libby Prison. The raid cost the life of Dahlgren, another gallant young cavalier. After Dahlgren's death, a Detroit newspaper reported, "[Kilpatrick] cares nothing about the lives of men, sacrificing them with cool indifference, his only object being his own promotion and keeping his name before the public."[20] Kilpatrick went on to command General William T. Sherman's cavalry forces in the western theatre and had a career as a diplomat after the war.[21] His dream of occupying the White House remained unfulfilled.

These three separate but closely related cavalry actions have been largely ignored by history. This happened even though three different soldiers were rewarded for their incredible bravery and outstanding service that afternoon. The reasons why are unclear. However, it is obvious that a division-sized counterattack by Federal cavalry paled in comparison to the drama of Pickett's Charge and the human wreckage left in its wake. While there are certainly examples of bravery and suffering on these three fields—after all, three Medals of Honor came out of these fights—they seem insignificant in the shadow of the grand assault that marked the High Water Mark for the Confederacy. J. E. B. Stuart, generally regarded as the role model for the Civil War cavalryman, once wrote, "All I ask of fate is that I may be killed leading a cavalry charge."[22] Eleven months later, Grumble Jones would fall in battle at Piedmont, doing just that.[23] This is precisely the sort of romantic and noble end that Elon Farnsworth met, but history has ignored it. Ironically, Capt. Kidd commented, "Farnsworth will not be forgotten as long as a grateful people remember the name and the glory of Gettysburg."[24] Instead, there are rampant tales that Farnsworth dishonored himself and the men he led by committing suicide. The heroism of the charge itself is all but lost to history today. It is time for those allegations to be put to rest and for this gallant charge to be remembered; the truth is that under other circumstances, Farnsworth's glorious charge would be as well-known and as revered as a similar and equally failed effort—the Charge of the Light Brigade—to which the mounted charge of July 3 is an excellent parallel.

It is also not currently acceptable to say that the Battle of Gettysburg continued after the retreat of the beaten Rebels from the clump of trees. All of the traditional accounts of the battle's climax end with the repulse at the stone wall, and with General Meade failing to order a counterattack. These versions of the story fail to account for the fact that a division-sized counterattack, supported by twelve pieces of rifled artillery, was made late in the afternoon of July 3. Failure to acknowledge this fact is disrespectful to the memories of the men, both Blue and Gray, who fought and died in these actions.

The National Park Service does little to encourage people to remember these fights. The area covered by Farnsworth's Charge has almost no interpretation other than the handsome monument to Williams Wells. South Cavalry Field has only a few monuments to the Regulars to indicate that a fight even took place there. The Wells monument sits alongside a main road, with no explanation, a mute reminder of a fight forgotten by time.

There is even less to see at Fairfield. While the battlefield itself remains in much the same condition as it was during the Battle of Gettysburg, only a dilapidated War Department marker and a small tablet placed in front of the Marshall house by the veterans of the 6th U. S. Cavalry give any indication that a bloody cavalry battle took place there late on the final day of the war's greatest fight. It is not romantic to dispel the notion that the battle ended with the repulse of the grand assault on the afternoon of July 3.

A number of Federal general officers lost their lives during the three-day conflagration in Pennsylvania. Only one fell inside enemy lines. Every one of them has a monument but Elon Farnsworth. The failure to recognize the bravery and gallantry of his futile charge is disrespectful to him and to the men who made it with him. In 1888, a monument to Farnsworth was proposed:

> ...to be placed on the spur of Round Top, southeast of Slyder's house, where he fell. It is to be composed of a mound of boulders gathered in the neighborhood, upon which is to be placed a pentagonal granite shaft, on each of the faces of which is to be inscribed historical data relating to the regiments of the brigade and battery engaged. The mound and shaft are to be surmounted by a statue of Farnsworth.[25]

Pleas went out to the veterans of his brigade to raise funds, because the planners wanted the monument to "be made one of the most striking features on the field, as his fall is one of the most romantic incidents of the battle of Gettysburg."[26] For reasons that remain unclear to this day, the monument never materialized, perhaps because the veterans were unable to raise the necessary funds to erect the monument. Like the charge that he led, a bold and fearless rider who met his death leading a futile but glorious charge, remains unlamented and largely forgotten by history.

Likewise in 1891, John B. Bachelder led the campaign to place monuments to the veterans on the battlefield at Gettysburg. He proposed placing a monument to the men of the 6th U. S. Cavalry on the battlefield at Fairfield. The regiment's alumni association encouraged the erection of a monument, and it had political support. In a letter to the *National Tribune*, Bachelder wrote:

> The selection of Fairfield from the long list of battles that the regiment participated in is partly due to its proximity to Gettysburg and its bearing on the result of Meade's great victory, and as the memorable spot on which the seven officers and 557 men of this famous regiment dashed with waving guidons and flashing blades on an advancing brigade—the flower of Stuart's cavalry. History tells the rest, Meade's flanks were saved, and Pickett charged. Gettysburg marked the turning-point in the war of the rebellion. The records of the regiment also tell that out of all the brave men who charged with Col. Starr at Fairfield, on July 4, 1863, only 84 men and one officer answered the bugle call at the setting of the sun.[27]

Bachelder concluded with an observation that remains true today, more than a century after his words were recorded:

> The National Government has done but very little to honor the unflinching courage and devotion of its little standing army, while the various loyal states have vied with each other in commemorating the deeds of their sons. Especially this is noticeable at Gettysburg, where the long rows of bronze and marble mementos point with pride to where each volunteer battalion fought, but nothing speaks of the Regular.[28]

While a monument was erected to each of the Regular units of the Reserve Brigade, the government's monument to the 6th U.S. stands along an unvisited stretch of the Emmitsburg Road, next to the position of Graham's guns, standing silent vigil but failing to tell the story of the men who fought and died at Fairfield. The regiment's veterans placed a small tablet in front of the Marshall house, but there is no recognition at all of the fight by the men of Jones' Brigade.

The regimental monument to the 5th U.S. Cavalry is badly misplaced, alone and desolate in a dense thicket nowhere near the spot where the 5th U.S. briefly got around the Rebel flank and into Robert E. Lee's rear. The monuments to the regiments of the Reserve Brigade and of Farnsworth's Brigade appear to have been placed in large part based on a crude map prepared by Confederate Brig. Gen. Jerome Robertson, who commanded Hood's Division at Gettysburg after Hood's fall. As a consequence, the monument to the 5th U.S. is largely lost today, and only a handful of visitors ever see it. It may be the least visited monument on the battlefield at Gettysburg. Some indication that this lonely monument stands in the woods should be placed on Ridge Road.

The National Park Service's lack of recognition that a counterattack indeed did occur is perhaps a reason for this neglect. The Park Service has done little to draw attention to the fact that a counterattack was launched and that, while unsuccessful, nevertheless pierced the Confederate line of battle and got around its flank.

The Union high command failed to follow-up on the opportunities created by the attacks of Farnsworth and Merritt. The high command squandered an unprecedented opportunity to destroy Robert E. Lee's army by failing to capitalize on the efforts of these brave Yankee troopers. No similar opportunity presented itself until the end of the war. A possible chance to end the war slipped through George Meade's fingers that afternoon, and the war continued for nearly two more years. This is perhaps the greatest irony and tragedy of the Battle of Gettysburg.

The second greatest irony and tragedy of the battle is the seeming unwillingness of the Park Service to recognize the efforts and sacrifices of these men. The irony lies in the fact that, if these attacks had been properly supported and coordinated, Robert E. Lee's army might have been driven from the field in wild rout. Had that occurred, Farnsworth's glorious charge would be remembered as the turning point of the war. Instead, it is a forgotten and forsaken chapter of the war, which has languished untold for far too long. This is a tragedy.

Epilogue

Today, we have the opportunity to pay appropriate tribute to the men, both Northern and Southern, who fought on the South Cavalry Field and at Fairfield. A beginning step is to turn on the lights on the National Park Service's Electric Map, to indicate that fighting took place after the repulse of Pickett's Charge. Doing so is historically correct and long overdue.

While budget constraints limit the National Park Service's ability to interpret these portions of the field, groups such as the Friends of the National Parks at Gettysburg provide funding and manpower for such worthy projects. Perhaps it is time for these organizations to get involved with such neglected portions of the battlefield. Another option worth consideration is the National Park Service's Adopt-A-Position program, wherein volunteer groups can "adopt" an important site and ensure its maintenance and continued viability for a two-year term. As of this writing, the sites where these units fought have not been adopted and are available for adoption. It is hoped this work will encourage readers to adopt some of the positions of the Federal units who fought on the South Cavalry Field and in Farnsworth's Charge, and to assure that they are kept well-maintained and attractive. Adding interpretation, in the form of wayside markers and plainly marked trails, would bring these important but forgotten fights to the position they deserve within Gettysburg historiography.

At the very least, the battered old War Department marker and the tablet erected by the men of the 6th U. S. at Fairfield should be refurbished. There should be some commemoration that two brave Regulars, one an Irish immigrant and the other a German immigrant, earned the Medal of Honor for their bravery there. Visitors would then know that something important happened on the trace of the Fairfield-Orrtanna Road that day. A wayside marker, strategically placed, would be a valuable addition, setting forth the facts to allow the tourist to understand what occurred there late in the afternoon of July 3, 1863.

Finally and most importantly, Elon Farnsworth deserves what his fellow fallen general officers already have—a monument commemorating his death in battle, while leading his veteran troopers in a glorious but hopeless charge which had endless promise and little impact in the long run. An organization called The Elon Farnsworth Memorial Association has been formed to accomplish this goal. Perhaps the Friends of the National Parks at Gettysburg and the good people of the state of Illinois can assist raising the necessary funds for erecting the monument to Farnsworth proposed by the men of his brigade during the 1880s. Doing so will finally give the fallen brigadier the respect so brave a man deserves for doing his duty in the face of great odds and giving the last full measure of sacrifice for the cause in which he believed.

Only then will the memories of the brave men who wore both the Blue and the Gray on the South Cavalry Field be properly served.

Monument to the 1st West Virginia cavalry.

Appendix — Order of Battle

The South Cavalry Field

Union
Army of the Potomac
Cavalry Corps
Maj. Gen. Alfred Pleasonton, Commanding

First Division (Brig. Gen. John Buford)
  Reserve (Third) Brigade (Brig. Gen. Wesley Merritt)
  1st U.S. Cavalry (362 officers and men)
  2nd U.S. Cavalry (407 officers and men)
  5th U.S. Cavalry (306 officers and men)
  6th Pennsylvania Cavalry (detachment) (242 officers and men)
    Total Strength: 1321 Officers And Men
    Losses: 49 killed, wounded, or missing.

  1st U.S. Artillery, Battery K (114 officers and men)
    Losses: 3 killed, wounded, or missing.

Third Division (Brig. Gen. Judson Kilpatrick)
  First Brigade (Brig. Gen. Elon J. Farnsworth)
  5th New York Cavalry (420 officers and men)
  18th Pennsylvania Cavalry (509 officers and men)
  1st Vermont Cavalry (600 officers and men)
  1st West Virginia (10 companies) (395 officers and men)
    Total Strength: 1925 officers and men
    Losses: 98 killed, wounded, or missing.
  1st U.S. Artillery, Battery E (61 officers and men)
    Losses: 1 killed, wounded, or missing.

Confederate
Army of Northern Virginia
First Army Corps
Hood's Division[1]

Law's Brigade (Brig. Gen. Evander M. Law)[2]
  4th Alabama Infantry
  15th Alabama Infantry

Robertson's Brigade (Brig. Gen. Jerome B. Robertson)
 1st Texas Infantry

G. T. Anderson's Brigade (Brig. Gen. George T. Anderson)
 7th Georgia Infantry
 8th Georgia Infantry
 9th Georgia Infantry
 11th Georgia Infantry
 59th Georgia Infantry

 Bachman's South Carolina Battery
 Reilly's North Carolina Battery
 Hart's Battery of South Carolina Horse Artillery
 1st South Carolina Cavalry (detachment of approx. 100 men)

The Battle of Fairfield

Union
Army of the Potomac
Cavalry Corps

First Division
 Reserve (Third) Brigade (Brig. Gen. Wesley Merritt)
 6th U. S. Cavalry (471 officers and men)
  Losses: 242 killed, wounded, or captured.

Confederate
Army of Northern Virginia
Cavalry Division

Jones' Brigade (Brig. Gen. William E. Jones)
 6th Virginia Cavalry
 7th Virginia Cavalry
 11th Virginia Cavalry
  Losses: 48 killed, wounded, or captured.
Chew's Battery (Capt. Roger Preston Chew)
  Losses: None.

Endnotes

Chapter 1

1. Edwin B. Coddington, *The Gettysburg Campaign: A Study in Command* (New York: Charles Scribner's Sons, 1968), 442.
2. *Ibid.*, 453.
3. Address of Col. Frederick C. Newhall, *Dedication of the Monument of the Sixth Penna. Cavalry on the Battlefield of Gettysburg* (Philadelphia: privately published, 1889), 12-13.
4. George William Watson, *The Last Survivor*, Brian Stuart Kesterson, ed. (Washington, WV: Night Hawk Press, 1993), 12.
5. John W. Busey and David G. Martin, *Regimental Strengths and Losses at Gettysburg* (Hightstown, NJ: Longstreet House, 1982), 103. The regimental strengths are as follows: 1st U.S., 17 officers and 449 enlisted men; 2nd U.S., 5 officers and 505 enlisted men; 5th U.S., 11 officers and 567 enlisted men; 6th U.S., detached to Cavalry Corps headquarters, and 6th Pennsylvania, 15 officers and 349 enlisted men.
6. Ezra J. Warner, *Generals in Blue* (Baton Rouge: Louisiana State University Press, 1964), 321.
7. *Ibid.*
8. Francis E. Heitman, *Historical Register and Dictionary of the United States Army*, 2 vols. (Washington, DC: Government Printing Office, 1903), 1:1029.
9. Sidney Morris Davis, *Common Soldier, Uncommon War: Life as a Civil War Cavalryman*, George H. Cooney, ed. (Bethesda, MD: SMD Group, 1994), 419.
10. *The War of the Rebellion: A Compilation of the Official Records of the Union and Confederate Armies*, 128 volumes in 4 series, (Washington, DC: Government Printing Office, 1889), Vol. 27, Part 1, 913. Hereafter cited as *O.R.*
11. Davis, 427.
12. E. R. Hagemann, ed., *Fighting Rebels and Redskins: Experiences in Army Life of Colonel George B. Sanford 1861-1892* (Norman: University of Oklahoma Press, 1969), 321.
13. Theophilus F. Rodenbough, "Some Cavalry Leaders," included in *Photographic History of the Civil War*, 10 volumes (New York, 1911), 4:271, 276 and 278.
14. J. H. Kidd, *Personal Recollections of a Cavalryman* (Ionia, MI: Sentinel Printing Co., 1908), 238-9.
15. Rodenbough, "Some Cavalry Leaders," 278.
16. *Indianapolis Daily Journal*, October 20, 1863.
17. Wesley Merritt, "Reminiscences of the Civil War," included in Theophilus F. Rodenbough, ed., *From Everglade to Canon with the Second Dragoons* (New York: D. Van Nostrand & Co., 1875), 294-295.
18. William L. Heermance, "The Cavalry at Gettysburg," in A. Noel Blakeman, ed., *Personal Recollections of the War of the Rebellion: Addresses Delivered Before the Commandery of the State of New York, Military Order of the Loyal Legion of the United States* (New York: G.P. Putnam's Son, 1907), 202.

19. *O.R.*,Vol. 27, Part 1, 923-924. For example, in one dispatch, Buford pleaded with Maj. Gen., John F. Reynolds, the commander of the Army of the Potomac's right wing, "When will the reserve be relieved, and where are my wagons?"

20. Samuel L. Gracey, *Annals of the Sixth Pennsylvania Cavalry* (Philadelphia: E.H. Butler & Co., 1868; reprint, Lancaster, OH: VanBerg, 1996), 178.

21. *O.R.*,Vol. 27, Part 1, 943.

22. Capt. Isaac R. Dunkelberger, "Reminiscences and Personal Experiences of the Great Rebellion," unpublished manuscript, Michael Winey Collection, United States Army Military History Institute, Carlisle, Pennsylvania.

23. The language of Pleasonton's order to Buford is interesting: "The Major General commanding directs me to order you to fall back to Taneytown and then to Middleburg, in case the enemy should advance in force upon you and press you hard. The cavalry will dispute every inch of the ground, and fall back very slowly to the point designated, and send in all information they can gather." *O.R.*, Vol. 27, Part 3, 470.

24. Warner, 266.

25. Edward G. Longacre, "Judson Kilpatrick," *Civil War Times Illustrated* 10 (April 1971), 25.

26. Warner, 266.

27. Willard N. Glazier, *Three Years in the Federal Cavalry* (New York: R. H. Ferguson & Co., 1873), 134-135.

28. Charles Francis Adams, *A Cycle of Adams Letters 1861-1865*, Worthington C. Ford, ed., 2 vols. (Boston: Houghton-Mifflin, 1920), 2:44-45. Adams also had little good to say about Cavalry Corps commander chief Alfred Pleasonton: "Pleasonton is, next to Hooker, the greatest humbug of the war." *Ibid.*

29. Longacre, "Judson Kilpatrick," 25.

30. Shelby Foote, *The Civil War: A Narrative*, 3 vols. (New York: Vintage Books, 1963), 2:572; George R. Agassiz, ed., *Meade's Headquarters 1863-1865: Letters of Colonel Theodore Lyman from the Wilderness to Appomattox* (Boston: 1922; reprint, Lincoln: University of Nebraska Press, 1994), 76.

31. *National Tribune*, September 15, 1892.

32. *Ibid.*, Busey and Martin, *Regimental Strengths and Losses*, 206.

33. Claudius Buchanan Farnsworth, *Mathias P. Farnsworth and his Descendants in America* (Pawtucket, RI: privately published, 1891), 94.

34. Warner, 148.

35. Faculty Minutes of the University of Michigan for May 3, 1858, copy in files at Gettysburg National Military Park; Manuscript by Col. John B. Bachelder, "General Farnsworth's Death," copy in files, Gettysburg National Military Park. This account indicates that "Two years later, the University was shocked by the news of a wretched carousal in which this young man was a leading spirit. One of the students lay dead at the coroner's rooms. Eight students were expelled, among them this man. On leaving the University he went to [Dr. Andrew D.] White [professor of history] and thanked him for what he had done for him, acknowledged the justice of the actions of the faculty, but expressed the hope that he would yet show that he could make a man of himself. Five years later that student fell at the head of his brigade at Gettysburg. It was Farnsworth. He made good his promise." There is no verification of this story available, other than this account.

36. Abner N. Hard, *History of the Eighth Cavalry Regiment, Illinois Volunteers, During the Great Rebellion* (Aurora, IL: privately published, 1868), 56.

37. Henry C. Parsons, "Farnsworth's Charge and Death," included in Robert U. Johnson and C. C. Buel, eds., *Battles and Leaders of the Civil War*, 4 vols. (New York, 1884-1888), 3:395.

38. Kidd, *Personal Recollections*, 162.

39. Hard, 76-77.

40. U. R. Brooks, *Butler and His Cavalry in the War of Secession 1861-1865* (Columbia, SC: n.p., 1909; reprint, Germantown, TN: Guild Bindery Press, 1994), 489-490.

41. Hard, 202.

42. Alfred Pleasonton to Brig. Gen. John Farnsworth, June 23, 1863, Alfred Pleasonton Papers, Manuscripts Division, Library of Congress, Washington, D.C.

43. Elon J. Farnsworth to John F. Farnsworth, June 29, 1863, Pleasonton Papers.

44. William C. Oates to Joshua L. Chamberlain, April 15, 1905, Trulock Collection, Pejepscot Historical Society, Brunswick, Maine. Oates stated, "...when my men were retreating... they encountered a thin line of dismounted cavalry men through which we ran and took two or three of them out as prisoners. About that I am not mistaken. They belonged to Kilpatrick's cavalry and we encountered them near the foot of Big Round Top, but made no halt, ran right through them and my men took two or three of them, as above stated, as prisoners, and from them we learned the command to which they belonged."

45. *O.R.*, Vol. 27, Part 1, 992.

46. *Ibid.*, 992-993.

47. *National Tribune*, September 15, 1892.

48. Sgt. Thomas J. Grier to John B. Bachelder, May 14, 1888, *Bachelder Papers*, New Hampshire Historical Society.

49. *National Tribune*, September 15, 1892.

50. John Hammond, "Memoir of the Battle of Gettysburg," *In Memoriam: John Hammond* (Chicago: P. F. Pettibone & Co., 1890), 60-61.

51. Grier to Bachelder, May 14, 1888.

52. Hammond, 60.

53. "General E. M. Law at Gettysburg," *Confederate Veteran*, Vol. XXX (1922), 50.

54. *Ibid.*

55. Ezra J. Warner, *Generals in Gray* (Baton Rouge: Louisiana State University Press, 1994), 175-6.

56. Harry W. Pfanz, *Gettysburg: The Second Day* (Chapel Hill: University of North Carolina Press, 1988), 254.

57. John L. Black, *Crumbling Defenses; or Memoirs and Reminiscences of John Logan Black, Col. C.S.A.*, E.D. Swain, ed., Brake Collection, United States Army Military History Institute, Carlisle, Pennsylvania, 36-7.

58. U. R. Brooks, *Stories of the Confederacy* (Columbia, SC: n.p., 1912), 260.

59. Brooks, *Butler and His Cavalry*, 177.

60. Brooks, *Stories of the Confederacy*, 260.

61. James P. Hart to John B. Bachelder, March 3, 1886, copy in files at Gettysburg National Military Park.

62. Brooks, *Stories of the Confederacy*, 282.

63. Although the Kern House has been altered, it still stands at the southwest corner of the intersection of Ridge Road and the Emmitsburg Road, about a mile or so south of the entrance to that portion of the National Military Park which includes the Round Tops. The Kern Farm sits across Ridge Road from a modern bowling alley.

64. Gracey, *Annals of the Sixth Pennsylvania*, 179-80.
65. William C. Oates, *The War Between the Union and the Confederacy and Its Lost Opportunities* (New York: Neale Publishing Co., 1905), 235.
66. John Singleton Mosby, *Stuart's Cavalry in the Gettysburg Campaign* (New York: Moffatt, Yard & Co., 1908), 18.
67. *O.R.*, Vol. 12, Part 2, 727.
68. Maj. Gen. J. E. B. Stuart to My Darling One, October 25, 1862, J.E.B. Stuart Papers, Virginia Historical Society, Richmond, Virginia.
69. Dobbie Edward Lambert, *Grumble: The W.E. Jones Brigade 1863-64* (Wahiawa, HI: Lambert Enterprises, Inc., 1992), 8.
70. Thomas W. Colley, "Brigadier General William E. Jones," *Confederate Veteran*, Vol. VI (1898), 267.
71. Lambert, *Grumble*, 4-6.
72. John D. Imboden, "Fire, Sword, and the Halter," *The Annals of the War written by Leading Participants, North and South*, from the *Philadelphia Weekly Times* (Dayton, OH: Morningside, 1988), 173.
73. Warner, *Generals in Gray*, 13-14.
74. *Ibid.*
75. *O.R.*, Vol. 27, Part 2, 760.
76. *Ibid.*, 752.
77. George M. Neese, *Three Years in the Confederate Horse Artillery* (New York: Neale Publishing Co., 1911), 188.

Chapter 2

1. Louis N. Beaudry, *Historic Records of the Fifth New York Cavalry* (Albany, NY: S.R. Gray, 1865), 63. This is a particularly interesting observation, because Chaplain Beaudry, the regimental historian was not even present at the time. He arrived after the charge was already over. Obviously, he depended on others to reconstruct this account. Louis N. Beaudry, *War Journal of Louis N. Beaudry, Fifth New York Cavalry*, Richard E. Beaudry, ed. (Jefferson, NC: McFarland & Co., Inc., 1996), 50.
2. *National Tribune*, August 25, 1887.
3. Personal Experiences of William Clay Potter (Capt. 18th Penna. Cavalry) in the Battle of Gettysburg, Civil War Collection, Musselman Library, Gettysburg College, Gettysburg, Pennsylvania.
4. Busey & Martin, 259. The monuments to both Elder's Battery and to the 5th New York Cavalry sit atop Bushman's Hill, nearly a quarter of a mile from the end of the charge, which took place on a spur to Big Round Top. This demonstrates just how far removed from the charge the New Yorkers were. Perhaps their participation might have made a difference to the outcome of the charge.
5. J. O. Bradfield, "At Gettysburg, July 3," *Confederate Veteran*, Vol. XXX (1922), 225.
6. W. T. White, "First Texas Regiment at Gettysburg," *Confederate Veteran*, Vol. XXX (1922), 185.
7. Recollections of A.C. Sims, Co. F., 1st Texas Infantry, Robert Brake Collection, U.S. Army Military History Institute, Carlisle, Pennsylvania. Capt.
8. Henry C. Parsons, "Farnsworth's Charge and Death," included in Robert U. Johnson and Clarence C. Buel, eds., *Battles and Leaders*, 4 vols. (New York: 1884-1888), 3:394.

9. Thomas L. McCarty memoir, copy in files, Gettysburg National Military Park.

10. H. W. Berryman to Dear Family, July 9, 1863, *New York Times*, July 3, 1913.

11. White, 185.

12. *Ibid.*

13. Berryman to Dear Family, *Ibid.*, James H. Henrick, Co. E, 1st Texas Infantry, to Dear Mother, July 8, 1863 ("Some of the regiment knocked them off of the horses with rocks"), copy in files, Gettysburg National Military Park.

14. Oates, *The War Between the Union and Confederacy*, 236.

15. Jeffrey D. Stocker, ed., *From Huntsville to Appomattox: R.T. Coles' History of 4th Regiment, Alabama Volunteer Infantry, C.S.A., Army of Northern Virginia* (Knoxville: University of Tennessee Press, 1996), 110.

16. Capt. William Porter Wilkin to his wife, July 31, 1863, *Athens (Ohio) Messenger*, August 13, 1863.

17. Potter memoir.

18. *National Tribune*, October 12, 1916.

19. Potter memoir.

20. *National Tribune*, October 12, 1916.

21. Stocker, *R. T. Coles' History*, 112.

22. *O.R.*, Vol. 27, Part 1, 1011.

23. Potter memoir.

24. Hammond, 61.

25. Account by Major John W. Bennett, 1st Vermont Cavalry, copy in files, Gettysburg National Military Park.

26. Hard, 259; Parsons, "Farnsworth's Charge and Death," 394; *National Tribune*, February 3, 1887; *O.R.*, Vol. 27, Part 1, 1005. There are many, many accounts of this exchange between Kilpatrick and Farnsworth. Most of them closely track Parsons' account of this discussion. However, one member of the 1st Vermont Cavalry, 1st Lt. Eli C. Holden, who served on Kilpatrick's staff, steadfastly held that there was no argument between the two generals that afternoon: "The discussion was continued amicably and courteously at intervals for more than an hour... Comrades, there was no quarrel between Gen. Kilpatrick and Gen. Farnsworth, July 3..." *National Tribune*, September 15, 1892. Unfortunately, the evidence simply does not support this conclusion. Rather, the volume of accounts which reference the loud disagreement between the two generals is overwhelming.

27. Howard Coffin, *Full Duty: Vermonters in the Civil War* (Woodstock, VT: Countryman Press, Inc., 1993), 199.

28. Nearly all of the accounts have the Texans overhearing this discussion. However, Col. Oates of the 15th Alabama contended that a member of the 4th Alabama Infantry overheard it. Oates, *The War Between the Union and Confederacy*, 236. This is the only such account that the author has seen.

29. John Purifoy, "Farnsworth's Charge and Death at Gettysburg," *Confederate Veteran*, Vol. XXXII (1924), 308.

30. H. Nelson Jackson, compiler, *Dedication of the Statue to Brevet Major-General William Wells and the Officers and Men of the First Regiment Vermont Cavalry on the Battlefield of Gettysburg, July 2, 1913* (privately published, 1914), 87.

31. Purifoy, 308.

32. *O.R.*, Vol. 27, Part 2, 400.

33. *Ibid.*
34. George Hillyer, "Battle of Gettysburg: Address Before the Walton County Georgia Confederate Veterans, August 2nd, 1904," copy in files, Gettysburg National Military Park, 13.
35. Parsons, 394-5.
36. Jackson, *Dedication*, 211.
37. Horace K. Ide, "The First Vermont Cavalry in the Gettysburg Campaign," Elliott W. Hoffman, ed., *Gettysburg Magazine*, No. 14 (1996), 16.
38. Bennett account.
39. Ide, 17.
40. Henry L. Benning, "Notes by General Benning on Battle of Gettysburg", *Southern Historical Society Papers*, Vol. 4 (1877), 177.
41. Ide, 17.
42. Account of Joe Allen, copy in files, Gettysburg National Military Park.
43. J. O. Bradfield, "At Gettysburg, July 3," 226.
44. "General E. M. Law at Gettysburg," *Confederate Veteran*, Vol. XXX (1922), 49-50.
45. Evander M. Law, "The Struggle for Round Top," in Robert U. Johnson and Clarence C. Buel, eds., *Battles and Leaders* (New York: Century, 1884-1901), 3:328.
46. J. O. Bradfield, "At Gettysburg, July 3," 236.
47. W. T. White, "First Texas Regiment at Gettysburg", 197.
48. Thomas W. Hyde, "Recollections of the Battle of Gettysburg," *Maine War Papers*, Vol. 1, Military Order of the Loyal Legion of the United States, read September 7, 1892, 199-200.
49. Jackson, *Dedication*, 88.
50. Evander M. Law to John B. Bachelder, June 11, 1876, *Bachelder Papers*, New Hampshire Historical Society.
51. Law, "The Struggle for Round Top," 3:329.
52. Stocker, *R. T. Coles' History*, 110.
53. *O.R.*, Vol. 27, Part 2, 391.
54. Stocker, *R. T. Coles' History*, 111.
55. *Ibid.*
56. Parsons, 395.
57. Stocker, *R. T. Coles' History*, 111.
58. Allen account.
59. Benning, "Notes", 177.
60. Coffin, *Full Duty*, 200.
61. Parsons, 395.
62. Allen account.
63. *National Tribune*, September 15, 1887.
64. Parsons, 395.
65. Sperry lingered until July 22, when he finally succumbed to his wounds. Jackson, *Dedication*, 47.
66. Parsons, 395.
67. Ide, 17.
68. Stocker, *R. T. Coles' History*, 112.
69. Col. William C. Oates to John B. Bachelder, September 16, 1888, *Bachelder Papers*, New Hampshire Historical Society.

70. Oates, 236.

71. William C. Oates to Edward Porter Alexander, August 25, 1868, Edward Porter Alexander Papers, Southern Historical Collection, The Library of the University of North Carolina, Chapel Hill, North Carolina.

72. Oates recalled it being just a "remnant" of the Federal cavalry force, and that it had been nearly "annihilated" by the time it reached his position. *Ibid.*

73. Parsons, 395.

74. *Ibid.*

75. *National Tribune*, December 3, 1891.

76. Ide, 17.

77. *National Tribune*, December 3, 1891.

78. Oates to Alexander, August 25, 1868.

79. Purifoy, 308.

80. *National Tribune*, September 24, 1891.

81. Oates to Bachelder, September 22, 1888.

82. Purifoy, 308.

83. There is no record of Farnsworth ever having been married. See Elon J. Farnsworth pension file, National Archives, Washington, D. C. His father filed the application as his surviving family member. See also, *Farnsworth Descendants*, 94.

84. Oates to Alexander, August 25, 1868.

85. G. G. Benedict, *Vermont in the Civil War: A History of the Part Taken by the Vermont Soldiers and Sailors in the War for the Union, 1861-1865*, 2 vols. (Burlington, VT: The Free Press Association, 1888), 2:602.

86. There is some controversy about where Farnsworth fell. The current position of the monument to the 1st Vermont Cavalry is not the original location. It was moved sometime in the 20th Century from a position about 150 feet to the north from where it stands today; the original foundation for the monument is still visible if one knows where to look for it. Many accounts have Farnsworth falling about 150 feet from the site of the 1st Vermont's monument. However, it must be remembered that most of those accounts were written before the monument was moved. Therefore, the author believes that the modern interpretations, which place Farnsworth's death site near the monument to Major Wells, are incorrect. Rather, the author believes that the actual site is at or very near the present-day location of the 1st Vermont's monument, which is surrounded by a triangular stone wall, much like that described in some of the accounts.

87. Parsons, 396.

88. *National Tribune*, December 3, 1891.

89. *Ibid.*, February 3, 1887.

90. *O.R.*, Vol. 27, Part 1, 1013.

91. Allen account.

92. Diary of George R. Crosby, entry for July 3, 1863, copy provided by Dr. Elliott W. Hoffman of Tiverton, Rhode Island.

93. Benedict, *Vermont in the Civil War*, 2:602.

94. Hillyer, 14.

95. Stocker, *R. T. Coles' History*, 112.

96. *O.R.*, Vol. 27, Part 1, 916.

97. *Ibid.*, 993.

98. *Ibid.*

99. *Ibid.*, 1005.

100. Alfred Pleasonton to John F. Farnsworth, July 15, 1863, Pleasonton Papers, Library of Congress, Manuscripts Division, Washington, D.C. Pleasonton, who was known to toady, may have been obsequious when he wrote this letter. Nevertheless, Elon Farnsworth had served on Pleasonton's staff, and Pleasonton had hand-picked the young captain for advancement, so it is quite likely that he felt remorse over the loss of a favorite aide.
101. *Pennsylvania at Gettysburg*, 2 vols. (Harrisburg, PA: B. Slingerly, 1904), 2:845-846.
102. James Longstreet, *From Manassas to Appomattox: Memoirs of the Civil War in America* (Bloomington: University of Indiana Press, 1960), 395.
103. Jackson, *Dedication*, 93. Felix Robertson eventually achieved the rank of brigadier general himself. Warner, *Generals in Gray*, 260.
104. *O.R.*, Vol. 27, Part 1, 1019.
105. William Wells to his parents, July 7, 1863, William Wells Papers, Bailey/Howe Library, University of Vermont.
106. Jackson, *Dedication*, 62.
107. Theophilus F. Rodenbough, "Cavalry Battles and Charges," in *Miller's Photographic History*, 4:234.
108. Parsons, 396.
109. *Ibid.*
110. *O.R.* Vol. 27, Part 1, 1009.
111. Law to Bachelder, June 13, 1876.

Chapter 3

1. William C. Oates to John B. Bachelder, March 29, 1876, *Bachelder Papers*, New Hampshire Historical Society.
2. In an 1868 letter to Longstreet's chief of artillery, Brig. Gen. Edward Porter Alexander, Oates wrote, "...His horse was killed and he fell, very badly wounded through the leg and thigh and one shoulder and in the abdomen. The lieutenant advanced towards him as he sat on the ground still grasping his pistol and again required him to surrender, to which he replied, 'I'll be damned if I do,' and placing the pistol to his own head, fired and shot his brains out." Oates to Alexander, August 25, 1868.
3. For example, in September 1888, while serving in the U.S. House of Representatives, Oates again reaffirmed this version of the story in a letter to Col. Bachelder. See letter of September 16, 1888, included in the *Bachelder Papers*. He related this account nearly verbatim in his 1905 memoirs. Oates, 236.
4. Oates to Bachelder, September 22, 1888.
5. For instance, this account is repeated almost verbatim in a 1924 article by John B. Purifoy which appeared in *Confederate Veteran*. See 309 of Volume XXXII of *Confederate Veteran*.
6. George T. Todd, "Recollections of Gettysburg," *Confederate Veteran*, Vol. VIII (1900), 240.
7. W. T. White, "First Texas Regiment at Gettysburg," *Confederate Veteran*, Vol. XXX (1922), 185 and 197.
8. J. O. Bradfield, "At Gettysburg, July 3," *Confederate Veteran*, Vol. XXX (1922), 236 (emphasis in original).
9. Recollections of A. C. Sims (Pvt., Co. F, 1 Texas) at the Battle of Gettysburg, Robert L. Brake Collection, United States Army Military History Institute, Carlisle, PA.

10. *National Tribune*, September 10, 1891.
11. Recollections of Capt. George Hillyer, copy in files Gettysburg National Military Park.
12. A. H. Belo, "The Battle of Gettysburg," *Confederate Veteran*, Vol. VIII (1900), 168.
13. Stocker, *R. T. Coles' History*, 112.
14. Benning, "Notes", 178.
15. Related in Rodenbough, "Cavalry Battles and Charges," *Miller's Photographic History*, 4:233-234.
16. Benedict, *Vermont in the Civil War*, 2:602-603.
17. *National Tribune*, September 24, 1891.
18. *Ibid.*, August 7, 1890.
19. *Ibid.*, September 15, 1892.
20. *Ibid.*, July 14, 1887.
21. Maj. Charles E. Capehart to John B. Bachelder, undated, *Bachelder Papers*.
22. Potter Memoir.
23. Parsons, 396.
24. Stocker, *R. T. Coles' History*, 112.
25. Kidd, *Personal Recollections*, 162.
26. Gerald F. Linderman, *Embattled Courage: The Experience of Combat in the American Civil War* (New York: The Free Press, 1987), 12 and 61-62. Linderman's underlying theory is that courage and its associated virtues of honor, duty, godliness, and knightliness were the motivating factors for soldiers of the Civil War, and that their underlying motivations were to demonstrate their courage in the face of horrible danger. Farnsworth appears to be an embodiment of this theory.

Chapter 4

1. Diary of Samuel James Crockett, Co. A, 1st U.S. Cavalry, Entry for July 3, 1863, copy in files at Gettysburg National Military Park.
2. Thomas J. Grier to John B. Bachelder, May 19, 1888, *Bachelder Papers*, New Hampshire Historical Society.
3. Dr. Samuel James Crockett to John B. Bachelder, December 27, 1882. The narrow deep creek which Crockett refers to is probably Marsh Creek, which flows in the area. Ridge Road passes over Marsh Creek in that part of the battlefield.
4. Gracey, 179.
5. Evander M. Law to John B. Bachelder, June 13, 1876, *Bachelder Papers*, New Hampshire Historical Society; Black, *Crumbling Defenses*, 41.
6. Harry W. Pfanz, *Gettysburg: The Second Day* (Chapel Hill: University of North Carolina Press, 1988), 254.
7. Newhall, *Dedication of the Sixth Pennsylvania*, 21. The Kern house has been altered, but it still stands at the southwest corner of the intersection of Ridge Road and the Emmitsburg Road, about a mile or so south of the entrance to the southern portion of the National Military Park which includes the Round Tops.
8. Gracey, 179.
9. Col. Laurin L. Lawson, *History of the Sixth Field Artillery, 1793-1932* (Harrisburg, PA: Telegraph Press, 1933), 57.
10. Black to Bachelder, March 22, 1886.
11. Dr. Samuel J. Crockett to John B. Bachelder, December 27, 1882.

12. Newhall, 21.
13. Dunkelberger, "Reminiscences."
14. Newhall, 21.
15. Lt. Eugene P. Bertrand to John B. Bachelder, March 26, 1864, *Bachelder Papers*, New Hampshire Historical Society. Bertrand's estimate of distance is inaccurate. It is more like 3.5 or 4 miles, not 1 mile.
16. *Ibid.*
17. Dunkelberger, "Reminiscences."
18. Crockett to Bachelder, December 27, 1882.
19. Black, *Crumbling Defenses*, 42.
20. Law, "The Struggle for Round Top", 3:328.
21. Crockett diary, entry for July 3, 1863.
22. Law, "The Struggle for Round Top," 3:327.
23. U. R. Brooks, ed., "Record of Hart's Battery From Its Organization to the End of the War," *Stories of the Confederacy* (Columbia, SC: 1912; reprint, Oxford, MS: Guild Bindery Press, 1991), 261.
24. Law, "The Struggle for Round Top," 3:328.
25. Dunkelberger, "Reminiscences."
26. Black, *Crumbling Defenses*, 42.
27. Lt. Eugene Bertrand to John B. Bachelder, March 26, 1864, copy in files, Gettysburg National Military Park.
28. It appears that Elder's Battery also contributed to this fight. Amateur archeologists have found fuzes, etc., from Elder's guns in the area, which support the contention that Elder's Battery did not spend the entire afternoon positioned at the point of its modern monument, atop Bushman's Hill.
29. Lawson, 57.
30. Merritt, "Reminiscences," 295.
31. Bertrand to Bachelder, March 26, 1864.
32. James F. Hart to John B. Bachelder, March 3, 1885, copy in files, Gettysburg National Military Park.
33. Law, "The Struggle for Round Top," 3:328.
34. *O.R.*, Vol. 27, Part 1, 74.
35. None of the accounts of the battle states this fact specifically. However, amateur archeologists have found Burnside carbine bullets alongside the position held by the 6th Pennsylvania. Author's interview with Charlie Tarbox, April 5, 1996. None of the units of Merritt's brigade used Burnside carbines. However, the 18th Pennsylvania was primarily armed with the Burnside, as was the 1st West Virginia. Busey and Martin, *Regimental Strengths and Losses*, 208. This is strong evidence to support the claim that the repulsed elements of Farnsworth's brigade fell into line with those elements of the 6th Pennsylvania holding an advanced position near the Kern house. No maps, however, show this position by the 18th Pennsylvania.
36. For more information regarding this charge, see Philip St. George Cooke, "The Charge of Cooke's Cavalry at Gaines Mill," included in Robert U. Johnson and Clarence C. Buel, eds., *Battles and Leaders*, 4 vols. (New York: Century, 1884-1888), 2:344-346.
37. For additional information, see Capt. James E. Harrison to Sir, June 16, 1863, James Harrison Papers, United States Military Academy Special Collections, West Point, New York, Reference No. 173.

38. Heitman, 1:695. In fact, Mason received a brevet to major for his gallant meritorious service at the Battle of Brandy Station.
39. Busey and Martin, *Regimental Strengths and Losses*, 258.
40. Temple Buford was the son of John Buford's older half-brother, Brig. Gen. Napoleon Bonaparte Buford. Temple was commissioned directly into the 5th U.S. in February, 1863, and served in the regiment for less than a year, before resigning his commission and enlisting in a Kentucky infantry regiment. After the war, he enlisted in the 1st U.S. Cavalry and served another 15 years, before retiring in 1882. Interestingly, later in life, Temple Buford filed for a veteran's pension, based on his participation in the fighting on South Cavalry Field. He claimed that he developed rheumatism as a result of his service at Gettysburg. The pension was eventually granted. Heitman, 1:260; Temple Buford Pension File, RG 15, The National Archives, Washington, D.C.
41. Gracey, 181.
42. *O.R.*, Vol. 27, Part 2, 400.
43. Evander M. Law to John B. Bachelder, April 22, 1886, copy in files at Gettysburg National Military Park.
44. Black to Bachelder, March 22, 1886.
45. Law, "The Struggle for Round Top," 3:327.
46. *O.R.*, Vol. 27, Part 2, 402-3.
47. *Ibid.*, 403.
48. *Ibid.*
49. J. Gary Laine and Morris M. Penny, *Law's Alabama Brigade in the War Between the Union and the Confederacy* (Shippensburg, PA: White Mane, 1996), 114.
50. Diary of Samuel J. Crockett, entry for July 3, 1863. Crockett has greatly overestimated the size of the opposing forces. At most, Merritt had 12 guns, not 20. Further, only four small Federal regiments were engaged in this action, and there was less than a full brigade of Confederate infantry involved in this engagement. While the numbers are a bit misleading, the description of the action is interesting and enlightening.
51. *O.R.*, Vol. 27, Part 2, 403.
52. This camp, of Kilpatrick and Merritt's commands, nearly wiped out farmer Houghtelier, whose estate later made a claim against the U.S. government for destroying acres of his farmland. For an interesting study of bureaucracy in action, see the claim file for the Houghtelier farm, National Archives, Microfilm Roll M-1093, Claim No. 214-703.
53. *O.R.*, Vol. 27, Part 1, 75.
54. *Ibid.*, 943.
55. Bertrand to Bachelder, March 26, 1864.
56. Busey and Martin, *Regimental Strengths and Losses*, 258.
57. *Ibid.*, 268.
58. Law, "The Struggle for Round Top" 3:329.
59. "Sketches of Hampton's Cavalry 1861-2-3," included in Brooks, *Stories of the Confederacy*, 178.
60. Newhall, 21.
61. Samuel J. Crockett diary, entry for July 3, 1863.

Chapter 5

1. War Record of Samuel H. Starr, July 13, 1892, The Samuel H. Starr Papers, Missouri Historical Society, St. Louis, Missouri.
2. Davis, *Common Soldier, Uncommon War*, 348 and 420.
3. *Ibid.*, 420.
4. James W. Milgram, "The Libby Prison Correspondence of Tattnall Paulding," *The American Philatelist*, 89 (December, 1975), 1114.
5. Charles F. Miller, "With the Sixth New York [*sic*] Cavalry in the Civil War," *Historical Wyoming Magazine*, 19, No. 2 (January, 1966), 38. Because this article is mistitled, it languished unseen for many years until the author unearthed it while researching this book.
6. Louis H. Carpenter, letter of July 13, 1863, Louis H. Carpenter, Letters from the Field, Collection No. A41-42, Historical Society of Pennsylvania, Philadelphia, Pennsylvania.
7. *Ibid.*, 41. Miller states that the man was in fact the infamous Confederate spy William Richardson, whom John Buford captured and hanged in Frederick, Maryland on July 7, on the retreat from Gettysburg. The author has been unable to confirm or deny this story.
8. Milgram, 1115.
9. *Ibid.*, 39.
10. William H. Carter, *From Yorktown to Santiago with the Sixth U.S. Cavalry* (Baltimore: Lord Baltimore Press, 1900), 97.
11. Davis, *Common Soldier, Uncommon War*, 427.
12. Milgram, 1115.
13. Miller, 39.
14. Davis, *Common Soldier, Uncommon War*, 348.
15. Carter, *Yorktown to Santiago*, 95.
16. Milgram, 1115.
17. Davis, *Common Soldier, Uncommon War*, 449.
18. *Ibid.*, 428-9.
19. *O.R.*, Vol. 27, Part 2, 752.
20. Davis, *Common Soldier, Uncommon War*, 436.
21. Henry B. McClellan, *The Life and Campaigns of Major-General J.E.B. Stuart* (Boston: Houghton-Mifflin & Co., 1885), 347.
22. T. J. Young, "The Battle of Fairfield, Pennsylvania," *Confederate Veteran*, Vol. V (June 1897), 251. This is one of the few good surviving Confederate accounts of this battle.
23. Milgram, 1115.
24. Davis, *Common Soldier, Uncommon War*, 431.
25. *O.R.*, Vol. 27, Part 2, 752.
26. *Ibid.*
27. *Ibid.*, 760.
28. William N. McDonald, *A History of the Laurel Brigade* (Baltimore: Sun Job Print Office, 1907), 155.
29. Davis, *Common Soldier, Uncommon War*, 431.
30. McDonald, *Laurel Brigade*, 155.
31. Richard L. Armstrong, *Seventh Virginia Cavalry* (Lynchburg, VA: H.E. Howard Co., 1992), 57.

32. *National Tribune*, September 17, 1891.
33. *O.R.*, Vol. 27, Part 2, 760.
34. *Ibid.*, 752.
35. *National Tribune*, April 30, 1891.
36. *Ibid.*, August 6, 1891.
37. John Blue, *Hanging Rock Rebel: Lt. John Blue's War in West Virginia and the Shenandoah Valley*, Dan Oates, ed. (Shippensburg, PA: White Mane, 1994), 203.
38. *Proceedings at the Fifth Annual Reunion of the Survivors of the Sixth U.S. Cavalry, Fairfield, PA, Tuesday, July 3, 1888*, Samuel H. Starr Papers, Center for American History, University of Texas at Austin, Austin, Texas, 5.
39. Neese, *Three Years*, 188-189.
40. Miller, 39.
41. Milgram, 1115.
42. William H. Carter, "The Sixth Regiment of Cavalry," *The Maine Bugle*, 3 (October, 1896), 299.
43. *Ibid.*, 300.
44. Mcdonald, *Laurel Brigade*, 155.
45. *National Tribune*, June 18, 1891.
46. *Proceedings at the Fifth Annual Reunion*, 5.
47. *O.R.*, Vol. 27, Part 2, 756.
48. Young, 251.
49. Blue, *Hanging Rock Rebel*, 203.
50. John N. Opie, *A Rebel Cavalryman with Lee, Stuart, and Jackson* (Chicago: W. B. Conkey Co., 1899), 178.
51. Blue, *Hanging Rock Rebel*, 203.
52. Opie, 172-3.
53. Blue, *Hanging Rock Rebel*, 203.
54. *Proceedings of the Fifth Annual Reunion*, 4.
55. Miller, 39.
56. Davis, *Common Soldier, Uncommon War*, 449-450.
57. *Ibid.*, 449.
58. *O.R.*, Vol. 27, Part 2, 756.
59. *National Tribune*, April 30, 1891.
60. Milgram, 1115.
61. Miller, 40.
62. Davis, *Common Soldier, Uncommon War*, 433.
63. *Ibid.*, 435.
64. Blue, *Hanging Rock Rebel*, 203.
65. Davis, *Common Soldier, Uncommon War*, 435.
66. William Harding Carter, *The Life of Lieutenant General Chaffee* (Chicago: University of Chicago Press, 1917), 31-32.
67. Carter, "The Sixth Regiment of Cavalry," 313.
68. Carpenter, *Letters from the Field*, letter of July 9, 1863.
69. Paul Shevchuk, "Cut to Pieces: The Cavalry Fight at Fairfield, Pennsylvania, July 3, 1863," *Gettysburg: Articles of Lasting Historical Interest*, 1 (July 1989), 113.
70. Carter, "The Sixth Regiment of Cavalry," 97.
71. Medal of Honor citation of Sgt. George C. Platt, The National Archives, Washington, D.C.

72. Milgram, 1115.
73. *Ibid.*
74. *O.R.*, Vol. 27, Part 1, 948.
75. *Ibid.*, 949.
76. Medal of Honor citation of Sgt. Martin Schwenk, The National Archives, Washington, D.C.
77. *O.R.*, Vol. 27, Part 1, 948. Mechanicstown is the modern town of Thurmont, Maryland.
78. Carpenter, *Letters from the Field*, July 9, 1863.
79. Blue, *Hanging Rock Rebel*, 203.
80. M. B. Carter, "Courier Kerfoot and His Deeds," *Confederate Veteran*, Vol. V (1897), 156-157.
81. McClellan, 348.
82. Carpenter, *Letters from the Field*, letter of July 13, 1863.
83. War Record of Samuel H. Starr.
84. Samuel Crockett diary, entry for July 3, 1863.
85. *National Tribune*, March 19, 1891.
86. *O.R.*, Vol. 27, Part 2, 754.
87. *Ibid.*, 760.
88. *Ibid.*, Part 1, 943.
89. Bertrand to Bachelder, March 26, 1864.
90. *National Tribune*, May 28, 1891.
91. *Ibid.*, June 18, 1891.
92. *Ibid.*, August 6, 1891.
93. *Ibid.*, June 18, 1891.
94. *Proceedings of the Fifth Annual Reunion*, 6.

Conclusion

1. Longstreet, *From Manassas to Appomattox*, 396.
2. Law, "The Struggle for Round Top," 3:329.
3. Address of Gen. Evander M. Law, included in Jackson, ed., *Dedication of the Statue to Brevet Major-General William Wells*, 90.
4. Benning, "Notes," 178.
5. John W. Phillips, "Address of Lieutenant Colonel John W. Phillips, Dedication of the Monument, 18th Pennsylvania Cavalry, September 11, 1889", included in *Pennsylvania at Gettysburg*, 2:890.
6. *Ibid.*
7. *O.R.*, Vol. 27, Part 1, 993.
8. *Ibid.*, 663.
9. Abner Doubleday, *Chancellorsville and Gettysburg* (New York: Charles Scribner's Sons, 1882), 202-203.
10. Diary of Silas D. Wesson, entry for July 5, 1863, *Civil War Times Illustrated* Collection, United States Army Military History Institute, Carlisle, Pennsylvania.
11. *National Tribune*, August 25, 1887.
12. T. M. Eddy, M.D., *The Patriotism of Illinois*, 2 vols. (Chicago: Clarke & Co., 1865), 1:558.
13. Kidd, *Personal Recollections*, 163.

14. Included in John Watts DePuyster, *Decisive Conflicts of the Civil War* (New York: McDonald, 1887); reprinted as *Gettysburg and After* (Gaithersburg, MD: Olde Soldier, 1987), 113. Writing years after the war, Pleasonton romanticized the exchange:

> From the suddenness of the repulse of the last charge of July 3d, it became necessary for General Meade to decide at once what to do. I rode up to him, and, after congratulating him on the splendid conduct of the army, I said: "General, I will give you half an hour to show yourself a great general. Order the army to advance, while I will take the cavalry, get in Lee's rear, and we will finish the campaign in a week." He replied: "How do you know Lee will not attack me again; we have done well enough." I replied that Lee had exhausted all of his available men; that the cannonade of the two last days had exhausted his ammunition; he was far from his base of supplies; and by compelling him to keep his army together, they must soon surrender, for he was living on the country. The General did not reply...

Alfred Pleasonton, "The Campaign of Gettysburg," the *Philadelphia Weekly Times*, included in *Annals of the War* (Dayton, OH: Morningside, 1988), 455-456.
15. Newhall, *Dedication of the Sixth Pennsylvania*, 21.
16. Crockett diary, entry for July 3, 1863.
17. Theophilus F. Rodenbough, "Cavalry War Lessons," *Journal of the United States Cavalry Association*, Vol. II (1889), 118.
18. Coddington, 525.
19. Oates, 45.
20. Detroit *Free Press*, March 26, 1864.
21. *O.R.*, Vol. 27, Part 2, 927. Special Order No. 113, which announced Kilpatrick's appointment to this task, was especially obsequious. It reads, "The gallant and distinguished Brigadier-General Kilpatrick, having tendered his services for a short period, is assigned to the command of the cavalry in the City of New York...." Distinguished is not a word often associated with an unsavory character like Judson Kilpatrick.
22. George C. Eggleston, *A Rebel's Recollections* (New York: Hurd & Houghton, 1875), 123.
23. For more on this largely forgotten battle, see, Scott C. Patchan, *The Forgotten Fury: The Battle of Piedmont, Virginia* (Fredericksburg, VA: Sergeant Kirkland's, 1996).
24. Kidd, *Personal Recollections*, 163.
25. The *National Tribune*, October 4, 1888.
26. *Ibid.*
27. *Ibid.*, March 19, 1891.
28. *Ibid.*

Appendix A

1. Reflects on those units engaged on South Cavalry Field.
2. Specific manpower and casualty figures on these regiments are unavailable because of the heavy casualties taken by them on July 2.

Bibliography

Primary Sources

Newspapers

Athens (Ohio) *Messenger*
Detroit *Free Press*
Indianapolis *Daily Journal*
The National Tribune
The New York *Times*
The Philadelphia *Weekly Times*

Manuscripts and other unpublished sources

Alabama Department of Archives and History, Montgomery, Alabama:
Robert T. Coles, "History of the 4th Regiment Alabama Volunteer Infantry, C.S.A., Army of Northern Virginia," 4th Alabama Infantry Regiment, Box 2.
Bailey/Howe Library, University of Vermont, Burlington, Vermont:
William Wells Papers
Gettysburg College, Gettysburg, Pennsylvania:
Personal Experiences of William Clay Potter
Gettysburg National Military Park, Gettysburg, Pennsylvania:
Joe Allen account
Maj. John W. Bennett account
Samuel James Crockett Diary
James Henrick letters
George Hillyer address
Recollections of Capt. George Hillyer
Thomas L. McCarty Memoir
Historical Society of Pennsylvania, Philadelphia, Pennsylvania:
Louis Henry Carpenter letters 1861-1864
Missouri Historical Society, St. Louis, Missouri:
Samuel H. Starr Papers
The National Archives, Washington, D.C.:
Record Group 15
Microfilm Roll M-1093, Claim No. 214-703
New Hampshire Historical Society:
John B. Bachelder Papers
Pejepscot Historical Society, Brunswick, Maine:
Trulock Collection
Pennsylvania State Library and Archives, Harrisburg, Pennsylvania:
Christian Geisel Letters

United States Military Academy, Special Collections, West Point, New York:
James Harrison Papers, Ref. No. 173

United States Army Military History Institute, Carlisle, Pennsylvania:
Civil War Times Illustrated Collection
Robert Brake Collection
Michael Winey Collection

United States Library of Congress, Manuscripts Division, Washington, D.C.:
Alfred Pleasonton Papers

University of Michigan, Ann Arbor, Michigan:
Faculty minutes of the University of Michigan

University of North Carolina, Southern Historical Collection, Chapel Hill, North Carolina:
Edward Porter Alexander Papers

University of Texas at Austin, Center for American History:
Samuel H. Starr Papers

Virginia Historical Society, Richmond, Virginia:
William E. Jones Papers
J.E.B. Stuart Papers

Articles

Belo, A. H., "The Battle of Gettysburg," *Confederate Veteran*, Vol. VIII (1900).

Benning, Henry L., "Notes by General Benning on Battle of Gettysburg", *Southern Historical Society Papers*, Vol. 4 (1877), 176-178.

Biddle, James C., "General Meade at Gettysburg," *The Annals of the War Written by Leading The Annals of the War Written by Leading Participants, North and South.* Dayton, OH: Morningside, 1988.

Bradfield, J.O., "At Gettysburg, July 3," *Confederate Veteran*, Vol. XXX (1922).

Carter, M.B., "Courier Kerfoot and His Deeds," *Confederate Veteran*, Vol. V (1897).

Colley, Thomas W., "Brigadier General William E. Jones," *Confederate Veteran*, Vol. VI (1898), 266-267.

Cooke, Philip St. George, "The Charge of Cooke's Cavalry at Gaine's Mill," included in Robert U. Johnson and Clarence C. Buel, eds., *Battles and Leaders of the Civil War*, 4 vols. New York: Century, 1884-1888, 2:344-346.

"General E.M. Law at Gettysburg," *Confederate Veteran*, Vol. XXX (1922).

Gregg, David McM., "The Union Cavalry at Gettysburg," *The Annals of the War Written by Leading The Annals of the War Written by Leading Participants, North and South.* Dayton, OH: Morningside, 1988.

Hammond, John, "Gettysburg Memoir", included in *In Memoriam: John Hammond.* (Chicago, P. F. Pettibone & Co., 1890).

Heermance, William, "The Cavalry at Gettysburg," included in Noel A. Blakeman, ed., *Personal Recollections of the War of the Rebellion: Addresses Delivered Before the Commandery of the State of New York, Military Order of the Loyal Legion of the United States*. New York: G.P. Putnam's Son, 1907.

Hyde, Thomas W., "Recollections of the Battle of Gettysburg," *Maine War Papers*, Vol. 1, Military Order of the Loyal Legion of the United States, read September 7, 1892, 199-200.

Ide, Horace K., "The First Vermont Cavalry in the Gettysburg Campaign," Elliott W. Hoffman, ed., *Gettysburg: Articles of Lasting Historical Interest*, No. 14 (1996).

Imboden, John D., "Fire, Sword and Halter," *The Annals of the War Written by Leading The Annals of the War Written by Leading Participants, North and South*. Dayton, OH: Morningside, 1988.

Law, Evander M., "The Struggle for 'Round Top'," included in Robert U. Johnson and Clarence C. Buel, eds., *Battles and Leaders of the Civil War*, 4 vols. New York: Century, 1884-1888, pp. 3:318-330.

Longstreet, James, "The Mistakes of Gettysburg," *The Annals of the War Written by Leading Participants, North and South*. Dayton, OH: Morningside, 1988.

Merritt, Wesley, "Personal Reminiscences of the Civil War," included in Theophilus F. Rodenbough, ed., *From Everglade to Canon with the Second Dragoons*. New York: D. Van Nostrand & Co., 1875.

Milgram, James W., ed., "The Libby Prison Correspondence of Tattnall Paulding," *The American Philatelist*, 89 (December, 1975).

Miller, Charles F., "With the Sixth New York Cavalry in the Civil War," *Historical Wyoming Magazine*, 19, No. 2 (January, 1966).

Newhall, Frederick C., "Address," *Dedication of the Monument to the Sixth Penna. Cavalry on the Battlefield of Gettysburg*. Philadelphia: privately published, 1868.

Parsons, Henry C., "Farnsworth's Charge and Death," included in Robert U. Johnson and Clarence C. Buel, eds., *Battles and Leaders of the Civil War*, 4 vols. New York: Century, 1884-1904, 3:393-396.

Pleasonton, Alfred, "The Campaign of Gettysburg," *The Annals of the War Written by Leading Participants, North and South*. Dayton, OH: Morningside, 1988.

Purifoy, John, "Cavalry Action Near Fairfield, PA., July 3, 1863," *Confederate Veteran*, Vol. XXXII (1932).

———, "Farnsworth's Charge and Death at Gettysburg," *Confederate Veteran*, Vol. XXIV (1924).

Rodenbough, Theophilus F., "Cavalry Battles and Charges," included in Miller's *Photographic History of the Civil War*, 10 vols. New York, 1911.

———, "Cavalry War Lessons," *Journal of the United States Cavalry Association*, Vol. II (1889).

————, "Some Cavalry Leaders," included in *Photographic History of the Civil War*, 10 vols. New York, 1911.

Todd, George T., "Recollections of Gettysburg," *Confederate Veteran*, Vol. VIII (1900), 240.

White, W. T., "First Texas Regiment at Gettysburg," *Confederate Veteran*, Vol. XXX (1922).

Young, T. J., "The Battle of Fairfield, Pennsylvania," *Confederate Veteran*, Vol. V (June 1897).

Books

Agassiz, George R., *Meade's Headquarters 1863-1865: Letters of Col. Theodore C. Lyman from the Wilderness to Appomattox*. Boston: 1922.

Alexander, Edward Porter, *Fighting for the Confederacy*, Gary W. Gallagher, ed. Chapel Hill: University of North Carolina Press, 1989.

Bates, Samuel P., *History of Pennsylvania Volunteers, 1861-1865*, 14 vols. Harrisburg: B. Singerly, 1869.

Beaudry, Louis N., *Historic Records of the Fifth New York Cavalry*. Albany, NY: S. R. Gray, 1865.

————, *War Journal of Louis N. Beaudry, Fifth New York Cavalry*, Richard E. Beaudry, ed., Jefferson, NC: McFarland & Co., 1996.

Benedict, G.G., *Vermont in the Civil War: A History of the Part Taken by the Vermont Soldiers and Sailors in the War for the Union, 1861-1865*, 2 vols. Burlington, VT: The Free Press Association, 1888.

Black, John L., *Crumbling Defenses; or Memoirs and Reminiscences of John Logan Black, C.S.A.*, E.D. Swain, ed. Macon, GA: J. W. Burke Co., 1960.

Brooks, U.R., *Butler and His Cavalry in the War of Secession 1861-1865*. Columbia, SC: The State Co., 1909.

————, *Stories of the Confederacy*. Columbia, SC: The State Co., 1912.

Cooney, George H., ed., *Common Soldier, Uncommon War: Life as a Civil War Cavalryman*. Bethesda, MD: SMD Group, 1994.

DePuyster, John Watts, *Decisive Conflicts of the Civil War*. New York: McDonald, 1867.

Doubleday, Abner, *Chancellorsville and Gettysburg*. New York: Charles Scribner's Sons, 1882.

Eddy, T. M., M. D., *The Patriotism of Illinois*, 2 vols. Chicago: Clarke & Co., 1865.

Eggleston, George C., *A Rebel's Recollections*. New York: Hurd & Houghton, 1875.

Ford, Worthington C., ed., *A Cycle of Adams Letters 1861-1865*, 2 vols. Boston: Houghton-Mifflin, 1920.

Glazier, Willard N., *Three Years in the Federal Cavalry*. New York: R.H. Ferguson & Co., 1873.

Gracey, Samuel D., *Annals of the Sixth Pennsylvania Cavalry*. Philadelphia: E.H. Butler & Co., 1868; reprint, Lancaster, OH: VanBerg, 1996.

Hagemann, E.R., ed., *Fighting Rebels and Redskins: Experiences in Army Life of Colonel George B. Sanford 1861-1892*. Norman: University of Oklahoma Press, 1969.

Hard, Abner N., *History of the Eighth Cavalry Regiment, Illinois Volunteers, During the Great Rebellion*. Aurora, IL: n.p., 1868.

Heitman, Francis E., *Historical Register and Dictionary of the United States Army*, 2 vols. Washington, D.C.: United States Government Printing Office, 1903.

History of the Eighteenth Regiment of Cavalry, Pennsylvania Volunteers, 1862-1865. New York, n.p., 1899.

Jackson, H. Nelson, ed., *Dedication of the Statue to Brevet Major-General William Wells and the Officers and Men of the First Regiment Vermont Cavalry on the Battlefield of Gettysburg, July 2, 1913*. Privately published, 1914.

Kesterson, Brian Stuart, ed., *The Last Survivor*. Washington, WV: Night Hawk Press, 1993.

Kidd, J.H., *Personal Recollections of a Cavalryman*. Ionia, MI: Sentinel Printing Co., 1908.

Ladd, David L. and Audrey J. Ladd, eds., *John Bachelder's History of the Battle of Gettysburg*. Dayton, OH: Morningside, 1997.

Longstreet, James, *From Manassas to Appomattox: Memoirs of the Civil War in America*. Bloomington: University of Indiana Press, 1960.

McClellan, Henry B., *The Life and Campaigns of Major-General J.E.B. Stuart*. Boston: Houghton-Mifflin & Co., 1885.

McDonald, William N., *A History of the Laurel Brigade*. Baltimore: Sun Job Print Office, 1907.

Meade, George G., *The Life and Letters of General George Gordon Meade, George G. Meade*, ed., 2 vols. New York: Charles Scribner's Sons, 1913.

Moore, James, M.D., *Kilpatrick and His Cavalry: Comprising a Sketch of the Life of General Kilpatrick*. New York: W.J. Widdleton, 1865.

Mosby, John Singleton, *Stuart's Cavalry in the Gettysburg Campaign*. New York: Moffatt & Yard Co., 1908.

Neese, George M., *Three Years in the Confederate Horse Artillery*. New York: Neale Publishing Co., 1911.

Oates, Dan, ed., *Hanging Rock Rebel: Lt. John Blue's War in West Virginia and the Shenandoah Valley*, Shippensburg, PA: White Mane, 1994.

Oates, William C., *The War Between the Union and the Confederacy*. New York: Neale Publishing Co., 1905.

Opie, John N., *A Rebel Cavalryman with Lee, Stuart, and Jackson*. Chicago: W. B. Conkey Co., 1899.

Pennsylvania at Gettysburg, 2 vols. Harrisburg, PA: B. Slingerly, 1904.

Pfisterer, Frederick, ed., *New York in the War of the Rebellion, 1861 to 1865*, 3rd ed., 5 vols. and index. Albany: J. R. Lyon Co., State Printers, 1912.

Rodenbough, Theophilus F., *From Everglade to Caxon With the Second Dragoons*. New York: D. Van Norstrand & Co., 1875.

Trout, Robert J., ed., *With Pen and Saber: The Letters and Diaries of J.E.B. Stuart's Staff Officers*. Harrisburg, PA: Stackpole, 1995.

Stocker, Jeffrey D., ed., *From Huntsville to Appomattox: R. T. Coles' History of 4th Regiment, Alabama Volunteer Infantry, C.S.A., Army of Northern Virginia*. Knoxville: University of Tennessee Press, 1996.

The War of the Rebellion: A Compilation of the Official Records of the Union and Confederate Armies, 70 volumes in 4 series. Washington, D.C.: United States Government Printing Office, 1889.

Secondary Sources

Articles

Carter, William H., "The Sixth Regiment of Cavalry," *The Maine Bugle*, 3 (October, 1896).

Longacre, Edward G., "Judson Kilpatrick," *Civil War Times Illustrated*, 10 (April, 1971).

Shevchuk, Paul, "Cut to Pieces: The Cavalry Fight at Fairfield, Pennsylvania, July 3, 1863," *Gettysburg: Articles of Lasting Historical Interest*, 1 (July 1989).

Wittenberg, Eric J., "Grumble Jones' Gettysburg Campaign Victory," *America's Civil War* (May 1997), 54-61.

——, "Merritt's Regulars on South Cavalry Field: Oh, What Could Have Been," *Gettysburg: Articles of Lasting Historical Interest*, 16 (January, 1997), 111-123.

Books

Allardice, Bruce S., *More Generals in Gray*. Baton Rouge: Louisiana State University Press, 1995.

Armstrong, Richard L., *Seventh Virginia Cavalry*. Lynchburg, VA: H. E. Howard Co., 1992.

Busey, John W. and David G. Martin, *Regimental Strengths and Losses at Gettysburg*. Hightstown, NJ: Longstreet House, 1982.

Carter, William H., *From Yorktown to Santiago with the Sixth U.S. Cavalry*. Baltimore: Lord Baltimore Press, 1900.

——, *The Life of Lieutenant General Chaffee*. Chicago: University of Chicago Press, 1917.

Coddington, Edwin B., *The Gettysburg Campaign: A Study in Command*. New York: Charles Scribner's Sons, 1968.

Coffin, Howard, *Full Duty: Vermonters in the Civil War*. Woodstock, VT: Countryman Press, 1993.

Encounter at Hanover: Prelude to Gettysburg. Hanover, PA: Hanover Chamber of Commerce, 1963.

Farnsworth, Claudius Buchanan, *Matthias Farnsworth and his Descendants in America.* Pawtucket, RI: privately published, 1891.

Foote, Shelby, *The Civil War: A Narrative*, 3 vols. New York: Vintage Books, 1963.

Forsgren, Leona Madora Farnsworth, *The Descendants of Moses Franklin Farnsworth.* N.P., 1972.

Freeman, Douglas Southall, *R. E. Lee*, 4 vols. New York: Charles Scribner's Sons, 1934.

——, *Lee's Lieutenants: A Study in Command*, 3 vols. New York: Charles Scribner's Sons, 1944.

Gallagher, Gary W., ed., *The Third Day at Gettysburg & Beyond.* Chapel Hill: University of North Carolina Press, 1994.

Hunt, Roger D. and Jack R. Brown, *Brevet Brigadier Generals in Blue.* Gaithersburg, MD: Olde Soldier, 1990.

Laine, J. Gary and Morris M. Penny, *Law's Alabama Brigade in the War Between the Union and the Confederacy.* Shippensburg, PA: White Mane, 1996.

Lambert, Dobbie Edward, *Grumble: The W. E. Jones Brigade 1863-64.* Wahiawa, HI: Lambert Enterprises, 1992.

Lambert, Joseph I., *One Hundred Years with the Second Cavalry.* Fort Riley, KS: Capper Printing Co., 1939.

Lawson, Col. Laurin L., *History of the Sixth Field Artillery, 1793-1932.* Harrisburg, PA: Telegraph Press, 1933.

Linderman, Gerald F., *Embattled Courage: The Experience of Combat in the American Civil War.* New York: The Free Press, 1987.

Longacre, Edward G., *The Cavalry at Gettysburg.* Lincoln: University of Nebraska Press, 1986.

Mitchell, Reid, *The Vacant Chair: The Northern Soldier Leaves Home.* New York: Oxford University Press, 1993.

Nesbitt, Mark, *Saber and Scapegoat: J.E.B. Stuart and the Gettysburg Controversy.* Harrisburg, PA: Stackpole, 1994.

Patchan, Scott C., *The Forgotten Fury: The Battle of Piedmont, Virginia.* Fredericksburg, VA: Sergeant Kirkland's, 1996.

Pfanz, Harry W., *Gettysburg: The Second Day.* Chapel Hill: University of North Carolina Press, 1988.

Price, George Frederic, *Across the Continent with the Fifth Cavalry.* New York: D. Van Nostrand, 1883.

Starr, Stephen Z., *The Union Cavalry in the Civil War*, 3 vols. Baton Rouge: Louisiana State University Press, 1976-1985.

Tucker, Glenn, *High Tide at Gettysburg.* Indianapolis: Bobbs-Merrill Co., 1958.

Warner, Ezra J., *Generals in Blue.* Baton Rouge: Louisiana State University Press, 1964.

——, *Generals in Gray.* Baton Rouge: Louisiana State University, 1959.

Waugh, John C., *Class of 1846.* New York: Warner, 1992.

Index

Adams, Charles Francis, 8
Adrian, John B., 36, 37, 45, 46, 48
Alabama Infantry regiments
    4th, 13, 22, 29, 32, 42, 48
    15th, 12, 13, 15, 38, 48
    44th, 13, 48
    47th, 13
    48th, 13
Allen, Joe, 28, 32, 33, 40
Anderson, George "Tige", 13, 54, 56, 67, 96
Artillery troops
    1st U. S. (Battery K), 3
    4th U. S. (Battery E), 9
    Bachmann's Palmetto (S.C.) light artil-
        lery, 14
    Chew's horse artillery, 18, 77, 88
    Hart's (S.C.) horse artillery, 14
    Rowan (N.C.) artillery, 14
Ashby, Turner, 17, 75

Bachelder, John B., 45, 101
Bachmann, William K., 14, 27, 33, 38, 49
Balder, Christian, 71, 72, 74, 81, 87
Belo, A. H., 48
Bennett, John W., 25, 28
Benning, Henry, 13, 33, 49, 93
Berryman, H. W., 21
Bertrand, Eugene P., 66, 89
Big Bethel, Va., battle of, 7
Big Pipe Creek, Md., 1
Big Round Top, 1, 12, 13, 20, 32-35, 48, 49, 69
Black, John L., 14, 53, 55, 56, 61, 66, 67, 95
Bradfield, J. O., 29, 46
Brandy Station, Va., battle of, 3, 4, 7, 10, 17, 61
Brigham, Loren M., 36
Brinkerhoff's Ridge, Pa., 2
Brown, W. J., 95
Buford, John, 2-7, 9, 17, 61, 95, 98
Buford, Temple, 61
Bushman Farm, 12, 60
Bushman's Hill, 60

Capehart, Charles E., 43, 50
Carpenter, Louis H., 84, 87
Cashtown, Pa., 18, 72
Chaffee, Adna R., 84
Chamberlain, Joshua L., 13

Chambersburg, Pa., 89
Charlton, Joseph, 80
Chew, Roger Preston, 18, 77, 88
Clark, Stephen, 36, 38, 39
Coles, Robert T., 32, 48
Committee on the Conduct of the War, 96
Confederate Veteran, 46
Connell, John B., 81
Connell, John H., 77
Cooke, Philip St. George, 4, 60
Cooper, George W., 89
Cram, George C., 71, 86
Crockett, Samuel, 55, 58, 64, 67, 96
Crosby, George R., 40
Cushman, Oliver T., 29, 32, 38, 51
Custer, George Armstrong, 8, 10, 95, 97
Custer's Brigade, 12

Davis, Sidney, 71, 82, 89
Devil's Den, 13, 29, 51
Devil's Kitchen, 35, 36
Doubleday, Abner, 94, 95
Doyle, Frank, 37, 50
Dulin, Billy, 10
Duncan, George H., 36
Duncan, R. R., 81
Dunkleberger, Isaac R., 6, 56, 58

East Cavalry Field, 8, 97
Edson, Ptolemy O., 43, 50, 51
Elder, Samuel K., 9, 20, 44, 58
Emmitsburg, Md., 6, 66, 87, 89
Emmitsburg Road, 7, 12, 15, 20, 23, 55, 58, 62, 64, 93, 101

Fairfield Gap, Pa., 18, 87, 97
Fairfield-Orrtanna Road, 71, 72, 74, 103
Fairfield, Pa., 16, 18, 19, 67, 69-74, 76, 84-90, 97, 98, 101, 103
Farnsworth, Elon J., 9-12, 20, 21, 23-29, 33, 38-46, 48-50, 52, 53, 60, 64, 67, 92-97, 100, 102, 104
Farnsworth, John F., 9, 10
Fluornoy, C. E., 18, 78
Freeman, David, 33

Gaines's Mill, Va., battle of, 60, 61
Gee, B. H., 62
Georgia Infantry regiments

About the Author

Eric J. Wittenberg is a practicing attorney in Columbus, Ohio. A native of Reading, Pennsylvania, he was educated at Dickinson College and the University of Pittsburgh School of Law. He has spent years studying Federal cavalry operations in the Gettysburg Campaign, with a special focus on the actions of Brig. Gen. John Buford and his veteran troopers. The author of a number of works on the mounted actions, he enjoys recounting the stories of the hardships faced by the cavalry forces of both sides in the American Civil War. He is a member of APCWS, the Brandy Station Foundation, and is a former president of the Central Ohio Civil War Roundtable. He is also the chairman of the Elon Farnsworth Memorial Association.

THOMAS PUBLICATIONS publishes books about the American Colonial era, the Revolutionary War, the Civil War, and other important topics. For a complete list of titles, please visit our web-site at:

http://civilwarreader.com/thomas

Or write to:

THOMAS PUBLICATIONS
P.O. Box 3031
Gettysburg, PA 17325